First World War
and Army of Occupation
War Diary
France, Belgium and Germany

47 DIVISION
140 Infantry Brigade,
Brigade Machine Gun Company
1 January 1916 - 28 February 1918

WO95/2732/3

The Naval & Military Press Ltd
www.nmarchive.com
Published in association with The National Archives

Published by

The Naval & Military Press Ltd

Unit 10 Ridgewood Industrial Park,

Uckfield, East Sussex,

TN22 5QE England

Tel: +44 (0) 1825 749494

www.naval-military-press.com

www.nmarchive.com

This diary has been reprinted in facsimile from the original. Any imperfections are inevitably reproduced and the quality may fall short of modern type and cartographic standards.

© **Crown Copyright**
Images reproduced by permission of The National Archives, London, England, 2015.

Contents

Document type	Place/Title	Date From	Date To
Heading	WO95/2732 47 Div Jan'16-Feb'19 140 Inf Bde MGC.		
Heading	47th Division 140th Infy Bde 140th Machine Gun Coy. Jan 1916-Feb 1918.		
War Diary	Sailly-La-Bourse	01/01/1916	02/01/1916
War Diary	Verquin	03/01/1916	03/01/1916
War Diary	Les Brebis	04/01/1916	12/01/1916
War Diary	Loos	13/01/1916	20/01/1916
War Diary	Les Brebis	21/01/1916	05/02/1916
War Diary	Loos	06/02/1916	14/02/1916
War Diary	Les Brebis	15/02/1916	15/02/1916
War Diary	Hautrieux	16/02/1916	29/02/1916
War Diary	Rupigny	01/03/1916	03/03/1916
War Diary	Coyecque	04/03/1916	08/03/1916
War Diary	Nedonchelle	09/03/1916	09/03/1916
War Diary	Ourton	10/03/1916	15/03/1916
War Diary	Gouy	16/03/1916	20/03/1916
War Diary	Ca Baret Rouge	21/03/1916	27/03/1916
War Diary	Gouy	28/03/1916	31/03/1916
War Diary	Carency Sector 1 Section at Bouvigny Huts 1 Section or Lorette Company, less 2 Sections, at Gouy-Servins	01/04/1916	07/04/1916
War Diary	1 Section in dug-outs at X.22.b.8.2 (map. 36c S.W 1/20.000) 1 Section in Cellars at Carency. Reminder of Coy. at Gouy-Servins	08/04/1916	30/06/1916
Heading	140th Brigade. 47th Division. 104th Brigade Machine Gun Company July 1916.		
War Diary	3 Sections in Souchez	01/07/1916	03/07/1916
War Diary	1 Section and H.Q. ataix-Noulette Transport at Hersin	03/07/1916	15/07/1916
War Diary	Hersin	16/07/1916	17/07/1916
War Diary	Berthonval Sector.	18/07/1916	24/07/1916
War Diary	Camblain L'Abbe	25/07/1916	26/07/1916
War Diary	Ourton	26/07/1916	27/07/1916
War Diary	La Thieuloye	28/07/1916	30/07/1916
War Diary	Wignacourt	31/07/1916	31/07/1916
Heading	47th Division. 140th Brigade Machine Gun Company August 1916.		
Heading	War Diary of 140th Machine Gun Company. From August 1st to August 31st, 1916. Vol 8		
War Diary	Wignacourt	01/08/1916	01/08/1916
War Diary	Boffles	02/08/1916	04/08/1916
War Diary	Le Festel	05/08/1916	05/08/1916
War Diary	Neuf Moulin	06/08/1916	15/08/1916
War Diary	Millencourt	16/08/1916	20/08/1916
War Diary	Bouchon	21/08/1916	21/08/1916
War Diary	Wagnies	22/08/1916	22/08/1916
War Diary	Mirvaux	23/08/1916	23/08/1916
War Diary	Franvillers	24/08/1916	12/09/1916
War Diary	Maxse Redoubt	13/09/1916	14/09/1916
War Diary	High Wood	15/09/1916	20/09/1916
War Diary	Becourt	21/09/1916	21/09/1916
War Diary	Henencourt	22/09/1916	31/10/1916

Heading	War Diary of 140th Machine Gun Company from 1st November, 1916 to 30th November, 1916. Vol XI		
Miscellaneous	H.Q. 140th Infantry Brigade	01/12/1916	01/12/1916
War Diary	Scottish Camp G.23.a.7.7 Map 28 N.W.	01/11/1916	30/11/1916
Miscellaneous	Appendix I (War Diary) 140 Machine Gun Coy November 1916		
Heading	Original War Diary of 140th Machine Gun Company from 1.12.16 to 31.12.16 Vol 12		
War Diary		01/12/1916	31/12/1916
Heading	Original War Diary of 140th Machine Gun Company from 1st January, 1917 to 31st January, 1917. Vol 13		
War Diary		01/01/1917	31/01/1917
Heading	Original War Diary of 140th Machine Gun Company from 1.2.17 to 28.2.17 Vol 14		
War Diary	Canal Sub-Sector Ypres	01/02/1917	28/02/1917
Heading	Original War Diary of 140th Machine Gun Company from 1st to 31st March, 1917. Vol 15		
War Diary		01/03/1917	31/03/1917
Heading	Original War Diary of 140th Machine Gun Company from 1st April, 1917 to 30th April, 1917. Vol 16		
Miscellaneous	H.Q. 140th Infantry Brigade.	03/05/1917	03/05/1917
War Diary		01/04/1917	30/04/1917
Heading	Original War Diary of 140th Machine Gun Company from 1st May, 1917 to 31st May, 1917. Vol 17		
War Diary		01/05/1917	03/05/1917
Miscellaneous	Canal Sub-Sector		
War Diary		04/05/1917	31/05/1917
Heading	Original War Diary of 140th Coy., Machine Gun Corps for June 1917. Vol 18		
War Diary	Dominion East Camp	01/06/1917	05/06/1917
War Diary	Coy. H.Q at Lock House	06/06/1917	07/06/1917
War Diary	Ypres. Spoil Bank Sector.	07/06/1917	12/06/1917
War Diary	Quebec Camp	13/06/1917	16/06/1917
War Diary	Ebblinghem	17/06/1917	28/06/1917
War Diary	Ypres (Ridge Wood)	29/06/1917	30/06/1917
Operation(al) Order(s)	140th Machine Gun Company Order No.9.	02/06/1917	02/06/1917
Miscellaneous	Appendix "A"		
Map	Map A Map No 12		
Heading	Original War Diary of 140th Machine Gun Company for July 1917. Vol 19		
Miscellaneous	Headquarters 140th Infantry Brigade	01/08/1917	01/08/1917
War Diary	Ypres (Spoil Bank Sector)	01/07/1917	04/07/1917
War Diary	Reninghelst	05/07/1917	07/07/1917
War Diary	Murrumbidgee	08/07/1917	08/07/1917
War Diary	Spoil Bank Sector	09/07/1917	23/07/1917
War Diary	Lion Camp	24/07/1917	31/07/1917
Heading	Original War Diary of 140th Company, Machine Gun Corps for August 1917. Vol 20		
War Diary	Lion Camp Sheet 28 SW. M.11.a.2.1.	01/08/1917	07/08/1917
War Diary	Ridge Wood	08/08/1917	12/08/1917
War Diary	Ascot Camp	13/08/1917	15/08/1917
War Diary	Etrehem	16/08/1917	21/08/1917
War Diary	St. Martin Au Laert	22/08/1917	24/08/1917
War Diary	Vancouver Camp	25/08/1917	27/08/1917
War Diary	Montreal Camp	28/08/1917	31/08/1917

Heading	Original War Diary of 140th Company Machine Gun Corps for September, 1917. Vol 21		
War Diary		01/09/1917	30/09/1917
Heading	Original War Diary of 140th Machine Gun Company for October 1917. Vol 22		
Miscellaneous	H.Q. 140th Infantry Brigade	01/11/1917	01/11/1917
War Diary	Field	01/10/1917	31/10/1917
Miscellaneous	Guns manned by 140th M.G. Coy, in Oppy sector during period 10th-26th October, 1917. Appendix 1.	10/10/1917	10/10/1917
Miscellaneous	Programme for the co-Operation of Machine Guns in the Raid by 17th Battn. Lon Regt., on the night 17th/18th October. Appendix 2.	17/10/1917	17/10/1917
Heading	Original War Diary of 140th Machine Gun Company for November 1917.		
Miscellaneous	HQ 140 Infantry Brigade	06/12/1917	06/12/1917
War Diary	Anzin-St-Aubin near Arras	01/11/1917	04/11/1917
War Diary	HQ at H5a55,65 Sheet 51B	05/11/1917	13/11/1917
War Diary	Railway Cutting B27a0.4 Sheet 51B	14/11/1917	17/11/1917
War Diary	Mont St Eloy	18/11/1917	20/11/1917
War Diary	Gouves	21/11/1917	21/11/1917
War Diary	Simencourt	22/11/1917	23/11/1917
War Diary	Courcelles-Le-Comte	24/11/1917	24/11/1917
War Diary	Beaulencourt	25/11/1917	25/11/1917
War Diary	Doignies	26/11/1917	28/11/1917
War Diary	Bourlon Wood near Cambrai	29/11/1917	30/11/1917
Miscellaneous	Ref Moeuvres 1/20000 M.G. Dispositions Sam 29.11.17	29/11/1917	29/11/1917
Heading	Original War Diary of 140th Machine Gun Company for December 1917 Vol 24		
War Diary	Bourlon Wood near Cambrai	01/12/1917	12/12/1917
War Diary	Bertincourt	13/12/1917	15/12/1917
War Diary	Coy HQ at K15d2.2 Sheet 57c	16/12/1917	20/12/1917
War Diary	Bertincourt	21/12/1917	22/12/1917
War Diary	Heilly	23/12/1917	31/12/1917
Miscellaneous	To 140th Inf. Bde. M.G. Dispositions	03/12/1917	03/12/1917
Miscellaneous	Casualties Killed		
Heading	Original War Diary of 140th Machine Gun Company for January 1918 Vol 25		
War Diary		01/01/1918	01/01/1918
War Diary	Heilly nr. Albert. (Somme)	02/01/1918	09/01/1918
War Diary	Heilly.	10/01/1918	10/01/1918
War Diary	Bertincourt.	11/01/1918	13/01/1918
War Diary	Ribecourt	14/01/1918	19/01/1918
War Diary	Map Ninewood 1/10,000	20/01/1918	25/01/1918
War Diary	Bertincourt	26/01/1918	03/02/1918
War Diary	Flesquieres Sector	04/02/1918	04/02/1918
War Diary	Ref Map Moeuvres	05/02/1918	15/02/1918
War Diary	Bertincourt	16/02/1918	23/02/1918
War Diary	Rocquigny	23/02/1918	28/02/1918
Miscellaneous	Positions of Guns Manned under the Winter Scheme in the Rifle Brigade Sector handed over by 140th Day MGC to 142nd Coy MGC	13/11/1917	13/11/1917
Miscellaneous	Operation Order No. 40 by Capt C.E.H. Druitt, M.C. Commanding 140 Machine Gun Company.	02/02/1918	02/02/1918
Miscellaneous	O. Order "A"		

WO95/2732

47 Div

Jan '16 – Feb '19

140 Inf Bde MGC.

(4)

47TH DIVISION
140TH INFY BDE

140TH MACHINE GUN COY.

JAN 1916 —   FEB 1918.

WAR DIARY or INTELLIGENCE SUMMARY

(Erase heading not required.)

Instructions regarding War Diaries and Intelligence Summaries are contained in F.S. Regs., Part II. and the Staff Manual respectively. Title Pages will be prepared in manuscript.

Place	Date	Hour	Summary of Events and Information	References to Appendices
SAILLY-LA-BOURSE	1/1/16		Guns in "D" Section (HOHENZOLLERN) 142nd Infantry Brigade on right flank. Casualties NIL.	
SAILLY-LA-BOURSE	2/1/16		Relieved by the machine guns of the 1st Div mounted Brigade.	
VERQUIN	3/1/16		142nd Inf: Brigade machine gun Company moved to VERQUIN. Casualties NIL.	
LES BREBIS	4/1/16		Machine gun Company moved to LES BREBIS. Casualties NIL.	
LES BREBIS	5/1/16		Formed line reconnoitred. Relieved by 35th French Brigade in the MAROC Sector. 141st Infantry Brigade on left, French on right flanks. Casualties NIL.	
LES BREBIS	6/1/16		Casualties NIL.	
LES BREBIS	7/1/16		Casualties NIL.	
LES BREBIS	8/1/16		Relieved by the 142nd Bde machine gun company during the day. Casualties NIL.	
LES BREBIS	9/1/16		Casualties NIL.	
LES BREBIS	10/1/16		Casualties NIL.	
LES BREBIS	11/1/16		Casualties NIL.	
LES BREBIS	12/1/16		Relieved 141st Infantry Brigade machine gun company in LOOS sector.	
LOOS	13/1/16		Casualties NIL.	
LOOS	14/1/16		Casualties NIL.	M.S.A.3½.2.
LOOS	15/1/16		Recce about north LOOS sector (LOOS- LAURENT road inclusive) Evacuated one other rank wounded. Casualties NIL.	G.36.D.4.2.
LOOS	16/1/16		Casualties NIL.	
LOOS	17/1/16		Casualties NIL.	
LOOS	18/1/16		Indirect machine gun fire directed on CITÉ ST PIERRE + tranche NE of DOUBLE CRASSIER. Casualties NIL.	
LOOS	19/1/16		Relieved by 142nd Inf: Brigade machine gun Company Casualties NIL.	
LES BREBIS	21/1/16		Casualties NIL.	
LES BREBIS	22/1/16		Casualties NIL.	
LES BREBIS	23/1/16		Relieved 140th Infantry Brigade machine gun company in the MAROC sector.	
LES BREBIS	24/1/16		Casualties NIL.	

WAR DIARY
INTELLIGENCE SUMMARY

(Erase heading not required.)

Army Form C. 2118

Instructions regarding War Diaries and Intelligence Summaries are contained in F. S. Regs., Part II. and the Staff Manual respectively. Title Pages will be prepared in manuscript.

140th INF. BDE. MACHINE GUN COY.

Place	Date	Hour	Summary of Events and Information	Remarks and references to Appendices
LES BREBIS	25/1/16		Intermittent shelling of LES BREBIS by light high velocity guns. Enemy aeroplanes very active. Casualties Nil.	
LES BREBIS	26/1/16		Slight shelling of LES BREBIS by light high velocity guns. Hostile artillery active on our front & support trenches. Casualties Nil.	
LES BREBIS	27/1/16		Intermittent shelling of LES BREBIS by light high velocity guns. Hostile artillery unusually active. Casualties Nil.	
LES BREBIS	28/1/16		Intermittent shelling of LES BREBIS by light high velocity guns. Front line supports & trenches very heavily bombarded by German guns. Lochnagar trench shelled by enemy at 6 P.M. enemy repulsed. 15th DIV: attacked by enemy at 6 P.M. enemy repulsed. Casualties Nil.	
LES BREBIS	29/1/16		Intermittent shelling of LES BREBIS by light high velocity guns. Hostile artillery not active. Casualties Nil.	
LES BREBIS	30/1/16		Atmosphere very misty. Reconnaissance impossible. Hostile shelling much less severe. LES BREBIS shelled by light high velocity guns. Road material gas shell poured into MAROC. Casualties Nil.	
LES BREBIS	31/1/16		Mist cleared. Heavily bombarded on evening of attack. Gas Shell perceptible in N. MAROC. Few S.A.A. S.E. bound. Casualties Nil.	

B. Baker Capt

WAR DIARY
INTELLIGENCE SUMMARY
(Erase heading not required.)

Army Form C. 2118

Instructions regarding War Diaries and Intelligence Summaries are contained in F. S. Regs., Part II. and the Staff Manual respectively. Title Pages will be prepared in manuscript.

140th INF. BDE. MACHINE GUN COY.

Place	Date	Hour	Summary of Events and Information	Remarks and references to Appendices
LES BREBIS	1/2/16		Relieved by 142nd Inf: Bde Machine Gun Coy at night. Fairly quiet day. Casualties NIL.	
LES BREBIS	2/2/16		Hostile aircraft were active. Casualties NIL.	
LES BREBIS	3/2/16		Casualties NIL.	
LES BREBIS	4/2/16		Relieved 141st Inf: Bde Machine Gun Coy in LOOS sector.	
LES BREBIS	5/2/16		at 15th Division on our own C.H. 1127,21f Brigade on our right flank. Company H.Q. in LOOS. S.E. wind new shafts believed issued, P.H. Tifer. Quiet day.	G35.B.1½.1½.
LOOS	6/2/16		Casualties NIL.	
LOOS	7/2/16		Hostile minenwerfer active. Casualties NIL. Quiet day. Hostile minenwerfer again active. Casualties NIL.	
LOOS	8/2/16		Quiet day. Hostile minenwerfer again active. CITÉ ST PIERRE Bardies. S.E. DOUBLE CRASSIER vicinity of FOSS 11 fired on by night by indirect M.G. fire. Casualties one other rank wounded.	M.6.c.8.8.
LOOS	9/2/16		5hoai, counter mine exploded by us a 1 A.M. Machine guns on flanks opened cross fire into general vicinity. Enemy tried to attempt to retire into to man the crater. No little activity. Fire on attempts to reserve. Enemy was quiet act. Casualties NIL.	
LOOS	10/2/16		W. wind. General aug is up. Casualties NIL.	
LOOS	11/2/16		Quiet day Casualties NIL.	
LOOS	12/2/16		Organised indirect Machine Gun fire at and CITÉ ST LAURENT. Casualties NIL.	
LOOS	13/2/16		Quiet day Casualties NIL.	
LOOS	14/2/16		Relieved by 3rd Inf: Bde Machine Gun Coy at night. Germans exploded a mine at 6.45 P.M., not much damage done. Two machine guns which were laid on the German line of the German line immediately opened up machine gun fire. Space between HARRISONS crater & the German line to man the crater, again when they retired to their own line. Germans advancing. Casualties NIL.	
LES BREBIS	15/2/16		Moved to HAUTRIEUX. Machine Gun Company at 3 hrs notice. Casualties NIL.	

Army Form C. 2118

WAR DIARY
INTELLIGENCE SUMMARY
(Erase heading not required.)

Instructions regarding War Diaries and Intelligence Summaries are contained in F. S. Regs., Part II. and the Staff Manual respectively. Title Pages will be prepared in manuscript.

Place	Date	Hour	Summary of Events and Information	Remarks and references to Appendices
HAUTRIEUX	16/9/16		Casualties Nil.	
HAUTRIEUX	17/9/16		S.H.Q. were ~~ordered to~~ warned to return at 9 hrs notice.	
HAUTRIEUX	18/9/16		Casualties Nil. S.H.Q. now in. Held in readiness to return at 9 hrs notice.	
HAUTRIEUX	19/9/16		Casualties Nil.	
HAUTRIEUX	20/9/16		Casualties Nil. Machine Gun Company at 1 hrs notice.	
HAUTRIEUX	21/9/16		Casualties Nil. Machine Gun Company at 3 hrs notice.	
HAUTRIEUX	22/9/16		Casualties Nil.	
HAUTRIEUX	23/9/16		Machine Gun Company in Corps reserve. General training carried out. Casualties Nil.	
HAUTRIEUX	24/9/16		General training carried out. Casualties Nil.	
HAUTRIEUX	25/9/16		General training carried out. Casualties Nil.	
HAUTRIEUX	26/9/16		General training carried out. Casualties Nil.	
HAUTRIEUX	27/9/16		General training carried out. Casualties Nil.	
HAUTRIEUX	28/9/16		Moved to RUPIGNY for training. Casualties Nil.	
HAUTRIEUX	29/9/16		Casualties Nil.	

BBarnes Lt-

Army Form C. 2118

WAR DIARY
or
INTELLIGENCE SUMMARY
(Erase heading not required.)

Instructions regarding War Diaries and Intelligence Summaries are contained in F.S. Regs., Part II. and the Staff Manual respectively. Title Pages will be prepared in manuscript.

[Stamp: 140th INF. BDE. MACHINE GUN COY]

Place	Date	Hour	Summary of Events and Information	Remarks and references to Appendices
RUPIGNY	1 Mch.		M.G. Coy in training area with 140 I.f. Bde. Section Training in the field. Attack practice.	Casualties nil. Fine
"	2 "		do. Training in use of machine gun.	do. Fine
"	3 "		Company Training. Attack scheme.	do. bgt. Shower
COYEQUE	4 "		M.G. Coy moved to new billets. Casualties nil.	do. Snow
"	5 "		Further Training. Attack on strong post. Practice night alarm - village patrol in state of defence.	do. Fine
"	6 "		Route March.	do. Wet
"	7 "		Attack practice. Use of gun & transport. Infantry crossing a river.	do. Frost
"	8 "		March to new billets.	do. "
NEDONCHELLE	9 "		Gun's classes rested in view of likelihood of move shortly.	do. Fine
OURTON	10 "			do. Snowy
"	11 "		"D" Section detached for duty with 15th Bn. move to BOUVIGNY HUTS.	do. "
"	12 "		" " " " " " LORETTE TRENCHES. byngy.	do. "
"	13 "		"A" " " " " 1st " " BOUVIGNY HUTS	do. "
"	14 "		M.G. Coy less 2 Sects. move up trenches & another M.G. Coy in support.	do. "
"	15 "		LORETTE TRENCH System reconnoitred. Casualties nil. FRONTLINE RIGHT reconnoitred.	do. Wet
GOUY	16 "		do. CABARET ROUGESPUR reconnoitred also Lefty frontline.	do. "
"	17 "		A Section to GOUY "C" Section relieve 141 M.G.Coy in Cabray.	do. "
"	18 "		Coy relieved 141 M.G.Coy in CARENCY Sects. { 2 gun Right and subs. Section 2 " Centre " " Support 2 " Left " " Front 2 " Left " " Support 2 " Cabaret Rouge Spur.	do. Fine
"	19 "			
"	20 "			
CABARET ROUGE	21 "		A Section relieved by 142 M.G. Coy moved to billets in ABLAIN.	do. do.
do	22		Casualties 1 Killed 2 wounded on Right gun. Team relieved resupplies made.	Wet.
do	23		Right Sub-Sector v ZOUAVE VALLEY reconnoitred with M.G. Coy on right flank.	Snow.
do	24		do	"

1875 Wt. W593/826 1,000,000 4/15 J.B.C. & A. A.D.S.S./Forms/C.2118.

Army Form C. 2118

WAR DIARY
INTELLIGENCE SUMMARY
(Erase heading not required.)

[Stamp: 140th INF. BDE. * MACHINE GUN Co.]

Place	Date	Hour	Summary of Events and Information	Remarks and references to Appendices
CABARET ROUGE	25th		Cavalier Hill.	
"	26 "		" Heavy rain.	
"	27 "		SOUCHEZ SPUR reconnoitred. Fine.	
"	28 "		M.G. Coy. relieved by 142 M.G. Coy. Line reconnoitred with incoming O/C Coy. Fine. Some rain. Cavalier Hill.	
GOUY	29 "		Cavalier Hill. Improvement of Billets. Hut-floors " Cavalier Hill. Fine	
"	30 "		" " Cook house erected " "	
"	31 "		" " Latrines " "	
"			" " Compound fenced in "	

B.B.Barnett

Army Form C. 2118.

Vol 4

WAR DIARY
or
INTELLIGENCE SUMMARY
(Erase heading not required.) April 1916 140th Machine Gun Company

Place	Date	Hour	Summary of Events and Information	Remarks and references to Appendices
CORENCY SECTOR	April 1		Machine Gun Company in Support. Casualties Nil.	
1 Section at BOUVIGNY HUTS	" 2		Pts Section detailed for meals in E. end of BOUVIGNY WOOD. Casualties Nil.	
1 Section on LORETTE	" 3		Reconnaissance of CORENCY SECTOR with OC 142 M.G. Coy. Casualties Nil.	
Company Hq 2 Sections at GOUY-SERVINS	" 4		Conference with OC 141 and 142 M.G. Coys.	
	" 5	Further	" " " " " " "	
	" 6		into 3 Sectors each allotted to a M.G. Coy - whose Guns are to be distributed in L.F.K.s, on festive purposes & are allotted to Front, Support and Reserve Brigades. By this means the Company relief, involving much labour at a bad period of the year, will be avoided; work should be more continuous and systematic and Guns will become more thoroughly acquainted with ground. Casualties Nil.	
	" 7			
1 Section in dugouts at K.22.L.8.1.2. (Map 36c S/20,000)	" 8		Night relief of 1 Section of 141 M.G. Coy by 1 Section 140th M.G.Coy. Casualties Nil.	
1 Section in cellars at CORENCY	" 9	7am	Reconnaissance of ZOUAVE VALLEY with OC M.G. Coy. on our right, with view to getting crossfire if necessary, along valley. Casualties Nil.	
Remainder of Coy at GOUY-SERVINS	" 10	5pm	Bombardment of PIMPLE by Heavy Artillery. Casualties 1 OR. Shell Shock	
	" 11		Not. Casualties Nil.	
	" 12		Not moving. Fire evening. Fired concealed enemy Trench emplacements in course of evacuation by M.G. Coy on right. Casualties Nil.	
	" 13	10pm	Reconnaissance of MAISTRE, OLD FRENCH and BOUGILLE lines. Gung to (a) weaken fire over enemy line from first and (b) approaches being used to front - advised that M.G. position in this line should be replaced by front personnel by sudden alarm. Casualties Nil.	
	" 14	5pm	Camouflet blown by us. Enemy galleries damaged - ours not broken. Enemy was nervous for cross fire. Enemy made a crack Rapid fire and supported. 1 Section (Russia cellars) again involved. Casualties Nil.	
	" 15		Fire. Enemy M.G. active on CABARET ROUGE & opposite Front tump enemy. Casualties Nil.	
	" 16		10ch. Enemy shelled right flank with gas shells. Casualties Nil.	
	" 17		10ch. Detail Examination of Frontline system of Battalion on right. Casualties Nil.	
	" 18		Not.	

2353 Wt. W2544/1454 700,000 5/15 D.D.&L. A.D.S.S. Forms/C.2118.

Army Form C. 2118.

WAR DIARY
or
INTELLIGENCE SUMMARY.
(Erase heading not required.)

140th Machine Gun Company

Instructions regarding War Diaries and Intelligence Summaries are contained in F. S. Regs., Part II. and the Staff Manual respectively. Title pages will be prepared in manuscript.

Place	Date	Hour	Summary of Events and Information	Remarks and references to Appendices
	April 19		Lieut. S. Burr stayed in BOTELLE Line Infantrie, at VILLERS AU BOIS "dugs table" designed for pivot of mounting, off-set to front of the bay to support. 2 miles down by Gunner on right. Enemy shelled ZOUAVE VALLEY and ERSATZ. Enemy M.G's active. Showery. Casualties Nil.	
	" 20		Inst. Inter. Sector relief. Casualties Nil.	
	" 21			
	" 22		Right Gun moved from Front Line to Support off ERSATZ. Consolidation of front of enemy trench line 2nd position, in work close to 2 platoons – ZOUAVE VALLEY trench fire. One Sergt Moncrieff wd. (by R.W.F.) 1 Sergt carried in. Resting party gave. Casualties Nil.	
	" 23		Inst. Right firing carried out from W. slope of ZOUAVE VALLEY in enemy trench. Casualties Nil.	
	" 24		Inst. Right firing carried out on 32nd. Casualties Nil.	
	" 25		Pr.i. 1 Section relieved from Souchez Comm. Casualties Nil.	
	" 26		Pr.i. At 3.45 p.m. mine blown by enemy in front of Brigade on our right – at 7 p.m. enemy barrage mistime. Enemy bombing attacks on Front Line made. Attack driven off. Casualties Nil.	
	" 27		Pr.i.	
	" 28		Pr.i. 1 a.m. Counter flare blown opposite centre battalion. 7.30 p.m. Enemy mine blown on right. No attacks followed. Casualties Nil.	
	" 29		Pr.i. Air blew mine opposite right battalion. CARENCY shelled. Casualties Nil.	
	" 30		Pr.i. Enemy mine blown at junction Front Line and ROBINEAU trench. Pr. S. Lt. ROBINEAU carried out effective fire on enemy Front Line trenches w/Lewis guns. Casualties 3 O.R. wounded. 1 O.R. killed.	

During the whole of this Month (a) The above weather conditions
(b) The isolation of the % of the units being made epidemic,
and (c) The Enemy mining activity, seriously retarded work on M.G. emplacements, most of which were in newly-dug and uncompleted trenches. In the circumstances, however, satisfactory progress was made.

B Barnes Capt.

WAR DIARY
or INTELLIGENCE SUMMARY

(Erase heading not required.)

Army Form C. 2118.

Vol 5   Nov 1916 / 140th Machine Gun Company

Place	Date	Hour	Summary of Events and Information	Remarks and references to Appendices
	May 1-12		During this period 140 M.G. Coy. occupied COBENCY SECTOR guns being placed as follows:— Post Guns Section 4 no's. to left of ERSATZ communication trench 1—GOBRON communication trench 1 in right and 1 on left COBURG communication trench — support line COSURG T. FIANQUEMENT 1 between ZOUAVE VALLEY between 130 trench & ERSATZ support line 2 — MAISTRE line 2. 6 in FRENCH BASTILLE line 2 MAISTRE line 2. The 142 M.G. Coy. held section on left. In combination with Infantry & Artillery, Barrage, night firing on enemy Batteries, roads & tracks was carried out nightly. The Company also worked in conjunction with 142 M.G. Coy. providing overhead fire from BRGAR ROAD in support of attack & raid on enemy lines made on my lot exploration of trenches. Attack was continued. The work of R.W.F. & machine gun party also on Western slope of ZOUAVE VALLEY was however, most hampered by frequent enemy barrages, adverse weather conditions and the friable nature of the soil. Casualties Nil.	
	13		Hostile mining activity, severe shelling by enemy during the evening. 1 O.R. killed.	
	14		Fair. Hostile mining activity. Conduct	
	15		Two Sections & trenches. Slopes of ZOUAVE VALLEY and in BASTILLE & MAISTRE line relieved by 141 M.G. Coy. Casualties Nil.	
	16		Remaining 4 Sections relieved by Section of 141 M.G. Coy. Casualties Nil.	
	17		Reconnaissance of BERTHONVAL SECTOR. 4 Lines of trenches in western slopes of ZOUAVE VALLEY visited viz. (a) Autos de la fosse by trained Guns. Guns rim four-infantry. There are much activity by Batteries of both. (b) A fortifiable single entrance unit damaged by hostile cross (c) Support line the TIN 2 which is in places in support line sheet cover, and in heavy pressure by Enemy too heated (d) the TIN 2 Newcomers line, in support line which in many peril contains in the trench and in the current of the trench. The trench and has been able of the removed soil of ditches by first fore finally not much trenches. These were worn deep stopes, but most of them had been all that sticky. All of the others are also supplied by Section 142 M.G. Coy. Relieved by Section 141 M.G. Coy. to BERTHONVAL Sector. 142 M.G. Coy. relieve Section of S. Support line. 1 in centre. 6 in Support line. 1 in Local reserve in Sector slope of ZOUAVE VALLEY. Casualties Nil.	
	18		Two Sections 140 M.G. Coy. relieved remaining Sections of 74th M.G. Coy. & 140 M.G. Coy. to 140 M.G. Coy. & 140 M.G. Coy. reserve dressed but as placed by 74th M.G. Coy. with well to the Rest Port 74th Ode. Shelters on western in front the gunnery to Berthonval by 74th M.G. Coy. Casualties Nil.	
	19		Heavy Enemy bombardment of Communication trenches & Supporting ranks attacks into 140 L. Ode took over fire fire Ode. Battalion both in order of attack by British front supports at Hospital fire of ERSATZ committee to take arriving on Left of Ode front Bypass phone in Support tie of to Section 342 to make air to L. Ode. advance to take arriving top of Fire L. Ode. Combined defense in Supply the Gun in ZOUAVE VALLEY on Western slope of 2 on trench nearer to GEARS ROAD. 1 O.R. wounded.	

WAR DIARY or INTELLIGENCE SUMMARY

(Erase heading not required.)

Army Form C. 2118.

Place: 140th Machine Gun Company.

Date	Hour	Summary of Events and Information	Remarks and references to Appendices
May 20		Relief of 174th M.G. Coy. at COMBLAIN L'ABBÉ taken over. Heavy Enemy T.M. bombardment of our line during afternoon night. Casualties Nil.	
21		Normal. Quiet. (1) Rifle entered bombardment lasting from 3.30 p.m. to 8 p.m. Enemy attacked MMY RIDGE & penetrated 3 lines of trenches. (2) Enemy bombardment & assault right of front repulsed by machine gun & rifle fire. Enemy driven back. (3) The Enemy attacked a weak & difficult advance followed by gunfire carried objective. (4) Barrage machine gun in position along GRUB ROAD was hostile instant fire on enemy & from casualties. Capt. B. BOWES wounded at early 11 am moving Coy. area. 2 O.R. wounded. 1 O.R. shell shock. 1 gun damaged.	
22		Ranged of a normal. 99th M.G. Coy took over relief. Lost 2 section 140th M.G. Coy. remained in line. Our returned area hours in ZOUAVE VALLEY at a section depot at a station on GRUB ROAD. Counter attacks by 140 Div. & 99th Bde. failed owing to heavy Enemy barrages & machine gun fire. Casualties Nil.	
23		Quiet day. Casualties Nil.	
24		2 Sections returned to billets at BRUAY. Casualties Nil.	
25		Posted in ZOUAVE VALLEY taken over by 99th M.G. Coy. and 140. M.G. Coy. moved to BAJOLLE LINE. Casualties Nil.	
26		Remaining 2 sections 140 M.G. Coy. removed from line. Casualties Nil.	
27		These two sections moved to billets at BRUAY. Casualties Nil.	
28-29		All M.G. equipment overhauled. recovery returns to rifles & specimens prepared. Casualties Nil.	
30		Inspection of Company by O.C. Casualties Nil.	
31		Brigade Command Parade. Casualties Nil.	

B. Barnes Capt.

Army Form C. 2118.

YM 6

140th Machine Gun Company.

WAR DIARY
or
INTELLIGENCE SUMMARY.
(Erase heading not required.)

Place	Date	Hour	Summary of Events and Information	Remarks and references to Appendices
	June			
	1-10		In billets at BRUAY. Section and Company training. Casualties NIL.	
	11		Recn. Reconnaissance of SOUCHEZ SECTOR. Casualties NIL.	
	12		Recn. Company moved to AIX NOULETTE & relieved 69th M.G. Coy in SOUCHEZ SECTOR. Line placed as follows:- KELLET Line 2. THE STRAIGHT 1. COMPANY FORD 1. HELMER Crater 1. Sunken Road 1. Ght. Road 1. In behind BOJOLLE Line 2. In reserve at AIX NOULETTE 8. 141 M.G. Coy on ANGRES SECTOR on right. 142 M.G. Coy on right on LORETTE. Casualties NIL.	
	13		Reconnaissance of MAISTRE LINE. Casualties NIL.	
	14		Registering scheme commenced.	
	15		Reconnaissance of MODELIN Trench & BOJOLLE line. Selection of positions (a) for night firing (b) for reserve guns in particular the ground in the neighbourhood of BRASS Road especially suited for all such fire zones to No Mans Land. Casualties NIL.	
	16		Night firing carried out from behind BOJOLLE & Sunken road on enemy. Casualties NIL.	
	17		Night firing carried out from behind BOJOLLE & Sunken road on enemy. Casualties NIL.	
	18		Casualties NIL.	
	19		Casualties NIL.	
	20		Casualties NIL.	
	21		Enemy bombarded KELLET Line with trench mortars. 1 O.R. shell shock.	
	22		Night firing for positions between ARRAS ROAD at Sunken Road on Enemy Salient opposite ANGRES SECTOR. Casualties NIL.	
	23		Casualties NIL.	

Army Form C. 2118.

WAR DIARY
or
INTELLIGENCE SUMMARY.
(Erase heading not required.)

140th Machine Gun Company.

Instructions regarding War Diaries and Intelligence Summaries are contained in F. S. Regs., Part II. and the Staff Manual respectively. Title pages will be prepared in manuscript.

Place	Date	Hour	Summary of Events and Information	Remarks and references to Appendices
	June 24		Enemy bombarded KELLET Line & the STRAIGHT. 1 O.R. killed	
	25		Casualties Nil.	
	26		R.G. fire on Enemy roads in LIEVIN which can be be enfiladed from ground in rear of H.Q. French.	
	27		Casualties Nil.	
	28		Casualties Nil.	
	29		Casualties Nil.	
			Night firing on Enemy communication trenches and roads opposite ANGRES Sector when ordered	
	30		To enfilade from SOUCHEZ SECTOR. Casualties Nil.	
			Casualties Nil.	

B. Barnes Capt.

140th Brigade.

47th Division.

140th BRIGADE MACHINE GUN COMPANY

JULY 1916:

WAR DIARY of INTELLIGENCE SUMMARY

Army Form C. 2118

140th Machine Gun Company

Place	Date	Hour	Summary of Events and Information	Remarks and references to Appendices
3 Sections at SOUCHEZ	1.7.16		Casualties Nil.	
	2.7.16		Casualties Nil.	
1 Section and H.Q.	3.7.16		Trench raid by 15th LONDON REGT. Ground prevented overhead fire in support but immediate area of salient raided but battery in action near ARRAS road fired into LIEVIN and 1 gun in front line on flank of attack swept enemy parapet opposite. Enemy M.G. in this position of trench did not fire. Casualties Nil.	
ITAIX—NOULETTE	4.7.16		A/c. Sector relief. No raid. 100% of emplacement in support line in position. Short hit by Trench Mortar. 1 OR wounded by mortar. Casualties Nil.	
Tangfort	5.7.16		Fine. No firing. Carried out, inspected enemy supply roads.	
	6.7.16		1 Officer killed.	
HERSIN	7.7.16		1 O.R. wounded. 1 O.R. returned to duty.	
	8.7.16		Sunny. 22nd LONDON REGT. raid on enemy salient opposite ANGRES Sector, Eastward M.G. fire maintained on enemy support lines, communication trenches and roads from SOUCHEZ for 30 secs. relief. Casualties Nil.	
	9.7.16		Fine. Sunny. 140th Bde Brigade held Conference of Kens Jun and M.G. Officers and devised to establish Brigade School. Casualties Nil.	
	10.7.16		Fine. Cool. Details for buying Machine Gunners at Brigade Shoot arranged. Casualties Nil.	
	11.7.16		Fine. Cool. Reserves to on 30 yds. range carrier out raid from motor trap. Scarcity found the fault. No report Nr. IV. T.O. shoots carried no appreciable retaliation in identification. Further experience with Company Rules—awry yard left. This method of laying gun for night or direct firing found to be as reliable as chronometer method. Also below nulls hazy or error negligible. Casualties Nil.	
	12.7.16		Rain in evening. Also below night. Series of tests of parties guns continued. Mean grain on Bull. Occasional examiners spotting table for photographic firing. My cause uncertainty was eye and procession nature of training. Casualties Nil.	
	13.7.16		Rain. Main Gun slightly damaged by shell. Casualties Nil.	
	14.7.16		Relief by M.M.G. Corps. Company moved to HERSIN to billets. Casualties Nil.	
HERSIN	15.7.16		BERTHONVAL Sector reconnoitred. Casualties Nil.	
	16.7.16		Fine. Company moved to GRAND SERVINS. 3 Sections reviewed 99th M.G. Coy. in BERTHONVAL Sector. All Guns in the line. Remainder of 1 Section in local at GOUY SERVINS. Casualties Nil.	
	17.7.16		Fine. Reserve and Reserve Sections relief to CAMBRAI L'ABBE and took over all M.G. positions.	
BERTHONVAL SECTR	18.7.16		Fine. 91st M.G. Coy. quiet day in trenches. Work started on dug-outs for all M.G. positions. New type of overhead cover emplacement devised and experimental emplacement started in ALHAMBRA redoubt. Casualties Nil.	

1875 Wt. W593/826 1,000,000 4/15 J.B.C. & A. A.D.S.S./Forms/C.2118.

Army Form C. 2118

WAR DIARY
or
INTELLIGENCE SUMMARY

(Erase heading not required.)

140th Machine Gun Company

Instructions regarding War Diaries and Intelligence Summaries are contained in F.S. Regs., Part II. and the Staff Manual respectively. Title Pages will be prepared in manuscript.

Place	Date	Hour	Summary of Events and Information	Remarks and references to Appendices
BERTHONVAL SECTOR	19.7.16		Fine. Night firing carried out from ANZAC road. Enemy M.G.s rather habitually fired. Stopped after our guns had fired about 15 minutes. Casualties NIL.	
	20.7.16		Fine. Casualties NIL.	
	21.7.16		Fine. Experimental emplacement finished after to-days work by 1 team of 6 - took two days to construct and included carrying materials. Casualties NIL.	
	22.7.16		Fine. Section in Reserve resumed section in front line. Casualties NIL.	
	23.7.16		Fine. 1 Section relieved by 1 section of 63rd M.G. Coy. Casualties NIL.	
	24.7.16		Fine. Remaining sections relieved by 63rd M.G. Coy. Casualties NIL.	
			Fine. Company in billets at CAMBLAIN L'ABBE. Preparation for move. Kit and stores reduced to minimum. Casualties NIL.	
CAMBLAIN L'ABBE	25.7.16		Fine. Company moved by march route to OURTON. Billets at Chateau for night of 26/27. 4 men casualties NIL	
OURTON	26.7.16		Fell out too exhausted but Mo.Ir. after arrival in billets. Casualties NIL	
	27.7.16		Fine. Company moved to LA THIEULOYE. 30 men fell out. Casualties NIL	
LA THIEULOYE	28.7.16		Fine. Day of possible future moves. Company carried out short training march followed by judicious rest in shade. Casualties NIL.	
	29.7.16		Fine. Day hot. Sections training in gun fighting. Experiments carried out with a view to using 4m.C. Battery in advance. Observed & unobserved telephonic communication. System of analysis of orders arrived at. New Vickers gun, to up now hastily received and tried. Ten conduct at Company Casualties NIL.	
	30.7.16		10 oclock. hurry to tog ay type from Casualties NIL. Day very hot. Company kind of march out to WGNSCOURT. No day march relieving voluntarily. No men fell out at arrival. Casualties NIL.	
WGNSCOURT	31.7.16		Fine. Day hot. Litho and company training in open fighting. Casualties and Consen labor of individuals at a Battery. Casualties NIL.	

Barnes Capt
O.C. 140th Machine Gun Company

47th Division.
140th Brigade.

140th BRIGADE MACHINE GUN COMPANY

AUGUST 1 9 1 6 ::

CONFIDENTIAL.

WAR DIARY

of

140th Machine Gun Company.

From August 1st to August 31st, 1916.

Army Form C. 2118.

W.D. E

WAR DIARY
INTELLIGENCE SUMMARY.
(Erase heading not required.)

140th Machine Gun Company.

Instructions regarding War Diaries and Intelligence Summaries are contained in F. S. Regs., Part II. and the Staff Manual respectively. Title pages will be prepared in manuscript.

Place	Date	Hour	Summary of Events and Information	Remarks and references to Appendices
	August			
WIGNACOURT	1		Fine. Very hot. Company moved to new billets at BOFFLES by march route. Casualties Nil.	
BOFFLES	2		Fine. Very hot. Training in open warfare continued. Scheme - R.F. Coy. in support of attack by Infantry on village, with special reference to movement of guns and consolidation of tactical points. Casualties Nil.	
"	3		Fine. Very hot. Company route march in light order from BOFFLES to WAVANS. Casualties Nil.	
"	4		Fine. Very hot. Company moved by march route to new billets at LE FESTEL. Casualties Nil.	
LE FESTEL	5		Fine. Cooler. Company " " " " " NEUF MOULIN. Casualties Nil.	
NEUF MOULIN	6		Fine. Hot. Company resting. Casualties Nil.	
"	7		Fine. Hot. Training continued - Special reference to siting guns in b action from bikes. Casualties Nil.	
"	8		Fine. Hot. Company trained with horsed transport in opening to artillery formation from column of route :- (a) along road with deep ditches or high hedges (b) along road with open space on one side (c) along road with open spaces on both sides. Coy. signallers cooperated in Brigade Visual Signalling Scheme. Casualties Nil.	
"	9		Fine. Hot. Training :- "Artillery Formations" continued. Box Respirators inspected by Divisional Gas Expert. Conference at 140 B.H.Q. - C.R.E. explained (a) principles of employment of R.E. and Pioneers in attack (b) Siting and construction of strong points. Casualties Nil.	

WAR DIARY
INTELLIGENCE SUMMARY

(Erase heading not required.)

140th Machine Gun Company

Army Form C. 2118.

Place	Date	Hour	Summary of Events and Information	Remarks and references to Appendices
NEUF MOULIN	August 10		Rain in morning. 2 Sections M.G. Coy. cooperated in practice attack on enemy trenches. Experimented with employment of 4 Guns in forward positions - e.g. shell holes in "no man's land" to support advance of Infantry. 2 practice attacks. Guns detached to accompany Infantry moved to flanks of each strong point. Nos. 1, 2 + 3 of gun teams instructed temporary position, remainder of team assisted R.E. by constructing M.G. position inside strong point. Cooperation with R.E. officer instructive. Casualties Nil.	
" "	11		Fine. Hot. Remaining 2 sections carried out training as noted for 10th August. Casualties Nil.	
" "	12		Fine. Hot. Training on range in morning - clearing stoppages, light operations - attack on trenches. The importance of holding some guns in local reserve, to substitute for any guns which may lose direction in the dark or become casualties, clearly seen, as difficulties of communication and advance are trebled in the dark. Casualties Nil.	
" "	13		Rain early. Fine later. Company Sports. Casualties Nil.	
" "	14		Showery. In morning - Machine Gun Company cooperated in Brigade attack on enemy trenches, ground particularly suitable for overhead covering fire, but "depth" of modern attack necessitates practice being as any high ground - otherwise probably before to have to leave our trenches the 1st wave may be approaching lower "safety angle". In evening - M.G.Coy. cooperated in Brigade T.M.Bs, rifle bombs and hand bombers practice attack on hostile system of trenches. Casualties Nil.	

WAR DIARY
INTELLIGENCE SUMMARY

(Erase heading not required.)

140th Machine Gun Company

Army Form C. 2118.

Place	Date	Hour	Summary of Events and Information	Remarks and references to Appendices
	August			
NEUF MOULIN	15		Showery. Company moved by march route to new billets at MILLENCOURT. Casualties NIL.	
MILLENCOURT	16		Fine, cooler. M.G. Coy. with Bde. on Brigade Route March. Casualties NIL.	
"	17		Showery, cooler. M.G. Coy. on range. Casualties NIL.	
"	18		Dull, cooler. Morning – M.G. Coy. on range. Conference in Bac Registrate at B.H.Q. with Chemical Adviser 4th Army. Casualties NIL.	
"	19		Hot. M.G. Coy. resting. Brigade Concentration march cancelled. Casualties NIL.	
"	20		Fine. Moon. Company moved to BOUCHON by march route. En route M.G. Coy. took part in Divisional Outpost Scheme. Under Brigade Orders / Section M.G. Coy. placed under orders of each Battalion. Sections employed by Battalions as follows:- 6th Bn. M.G. kept in reserve. 7th Bn. M.G. used in pairs in piquet-line – active filling left to Section Officers. 8 Bn. 3 guns in piquet-line, 1 Gun in support. Actual filling left to Section Officers. 15th Battalion – 1 gun allotted to each Company. Be Company Commander allotted his Section to 1 platoon. Casualties NIL.	
BOUCHON	21		Fine. Moon. Company move by march route to WAGNIES. Casualties NIL.	
WAGNIES	22		Fine. Company moved by march route to MIRVAUX. Casualties NIL.	
MIRVAUX	23		Fine, cool. Company moved by march route to FRANVILLERS. Casualties NIL.	
FRANVILLERS	24		Fine, cool. Elementary training. Review of mechanism, stoppages etc. Reconnaissance of country by Section officers. Casualties NIL.	

Army Form C. 2118.

WAR DIARY

INTELLIGENCE SUMMARY

(Erase heading not required.)

140th Machine Gun Company

Instructions regarding War Diaries and Intelligence Summaries are contained in F.S. Regs., Part II. and the Staff Manual respectively. Title pages will be prepared in manuscript.

Place	Date	Hour	Summary of Events and Information	Remarks and references to Appendices
FRANVILLERS	August 25		Fine. Morn. Instruction in bombing by B.G.O. Instruction in the construction of implements in strong point. Casualties. 1 O.R. accidentally injured.	
"	26		Rain. Rigging implements for strong points. N.C.O's instruction in use of prismatic compass. Reconnaissance of routes up to Left Division (III Corps) front – main C.T.S., Reserve Line and rearward defence and posts of Brigade H.Q. Casualties Nil.	
"	27		Rain. Company resting. Reconnaissance of routes up to Right Division (III Corps) front – main C.T.S., Reserve Line, Rearward defences & position of Brigade H.Q. Casualties Nil.	
"	28		Rain. Company went to rest. Coy. Signallers cooperated in Brigade Signal Scheme. Casualties Nil.	
"	29		Rain. Company on range. Casualties Nil.	
"	30		Rain. Gun equipment overhauled. Casualties Nil.	
"	31		Fair. Company went back. Reconnaissance by O.C. "B" Section and Transport Officer of routes up to Right Division (III Corps) front – main C.T.S., Reserve Line, Rearward defences & position of Brigade H.Q. also disposition (Sound) of 3 Machine Gun Companies of the Division. 1 Officer & 20 O.R. attended Fourth Army Gun School – demonstration. Casualties Nil.	

B. Bane? Capt.
OC 140 Machine Gun Company

WAR DIARY
INTELLIGENCE SUMMARY

(Erase heading not required.)

Army Form C. 2118.

Original
WD.9
140th Machine Gun Company

Place	Date	Hour	Summary of Events and Information	Remarks and references to Appendices
FRANVILLERS	Sept. 1		Fine. Company exercised in jigging and method of "quick release." Experiments carried out with Subsection Dials and ABNEY Level & BARR and STROUD rangefinder – Enclosure – Characteristic on T/S machinable over 900x. Casualties Nil.	
"	2		Fine – Morning. Organised attack practice – 2 Sections in position for covering fire. 1 Section advanced to attack point at farm between + O.G.2 + O.G.3 – ½ Section to support O.P.1 and support – ½ Section remained in reserve. Company meeting. Casualties Nil.	
"	3		Fine morning. Wet evening. Company meeting.	
"	4		Wet. Practice in rapid adjustment of gas helmets. Key tests for advanced training. Elementary training in stoppages and mechanism carried on in billets. Quick release practised in yards. Casualties Nil.	
"	5		Dull. Col. M. arrived in Coy & Lieut. Port moved out to. CO's lecture to officers and NCOs on indirect fire and time of flight. Casualties Nil.	
"	6		Fine. Several exercises of flagged covered (HIGH WOOD) warning Coy experiments with 140 Lgt. Bde. in ½pt. 1 Section in "HIGH WOOD" moved forward as soon as high ground as captured. Others attached to Battalion attacking & supporting just Communication duties. 3 Sections in Reserve. After high & Second Objectives 3 Others moved up and carried on overhead covering fire. 1 Section remained in reserve. Casualties Nil.	
"	7		Fine. Reconnoitred 1st Division Front by O.C. Coy. and O.C. A Section. HIGH WOOD, BAZENTIN-L-G_AND and area in rear with special reference to:- ① Transport Routes ② Gun Emplacements ③ Communication Trenches ④ Dumps ⑤ Section of M.G.Coy + Brigade. ⑥ H.Q. and advances and Observation. H.Q. ⑦ Suggestions (available) of M.G. Coys. Company Route March. Casualties Nil.	
"	8		Fine. M.G.Coy. exercised in attack over flagged course by Divisions given on the Official Officers (C + D Battns) accompanied the line. Casualties Nil.	

Army Form C. 2118.

Original

WAR DIARY
or
INTELLIGENCE SUMMARY

(Erase heading not required.)

Instructions regarding War Diaries and Intelligence Summaries are contained in F. S. Regs., Part II and the Staff Manual respectively. Title Pages will be prepared in manuscript.

H.Q. 5 Machine Gun Company.

Place	Date	Hour	Summary of Events and Information	Remarks and references to Appendices
FRANVILLERS	Sept 9		Fine. Company practised in advance in artillery formation and taking up positions.	Casualties Nil
	10		Dull. Church Parade.	Casualties Nil
	11		Dull Showery. Preparations for line. Lewis Lecture conducted etc	Casualties Nil
	12		Showery. Company moved by March route to MAXSE REDOUBT. M.G.Coy in reserve	
MAXSE REDOUBT	13		to O.C. 6y 142 B/T. Reconnoitred line.	Casualties Nil
~~FOURVILLIERS~~			Fine. Cold. Company moved to line. Location to front line remaining 3 sections in reserve at BAZENTIN LE GRAND. Heavy enemy shelling along afternoon. HIGH WOOD heavily shelled from 11am - 2pm and 4pm - 10pm. Aeroplane fight down our balloon about 7pm.	
	14		Casualties. Wounded Lieut B. BARNEY & 3 O.R. Killed 2 O.R. Fine. 47th Division attacked German lines in HIGH WOOD at 6.20am. 140th Brigade on right captured 1st objectives. Attack by 141 Brigade held up on left of HIGH WOOD. SWITCH LINE and FLERS (C) sent only after 1st 3 sections M.G. Coy carried out intense overhead indirect fire on SWITCH LINE in direction of FLERS. 3 Lewis Vickers support from 6.20am to 6.25am. 12,000 rounds fired. 1 section objectives had been taken and took up positions. 1 section in direction SWITCH LINE and HIGH WOOD in direction of MARTINPUICH ROAD - position approximately junction SUNK ROAD. 1 Section. Supporting to O.B.1. in HIGH WOOD at F.32 am.	Casualties Nil
HIGH WOOD	15		Casualties. Wounded 2 O.R. H.S.HEWETT & 6 O.R. PRATT and 6 O.R. 2 guns (C Section) on left of SWITCH LINE moved with teams. Officer & infantry referred to. Casualties killed 5 O.R. wounded 9 O.R. Missing 5 O.R. by Mr. M. G. Coy at night	Casualties Nil
	16		Fine. 1 Section taken down to battery positions as reserve.	
	17		Fine. German COUGH DROP disposed party of enemy which approached position in afternoon. 2 guns moved up to STARFISH in evening. Minimum ammunition can now up	
	18		to support BAZENTIN-LE-GRAND heavily shelled by star shells at night. Coy transfer and rations moved to BOTTOM WOOD. Casualties Nil by day. Artillery quiet. 4 guns moved up to a position in rear of STARFISH at night. O.C. reconnoitred line.	Casualties Nil

2449 Wt. W14957/M90 750,000 1/16 J.B.C. & A. Forms/C.2118/12.

Army Form C. 2118.

Original

WAR DIARY
or
INTELLIGENCE SUMMARY
(Erase heading not required.)

140 Machine Gun Company

Instructions regarding War Diaries and Intelligence Summaries are contained in F. S. Regs., Part II. and the Staff Manual respectively. Title Pages will be prepared in manuscript.

Place	Date	Hour	Summary of Events and Information	Remarks and references to Appendices
HIGH WOOD	September 19		Rain. Section in position in rear of STARFISH moved up to the redoubt.	
		6pm	Enemy counter bombs attack on DROP ALLEY. 1st M.G. Coy relieved 3 sections of my Ft. Casualties. WOUNDED 2/Lt W.F. CATTON and S.P.R.	
	20		Rain. Remaining section relieved by section of 1st S.A. G. Coy & early morning. Coy. resting at BECOURT. Transport at BOTTOM WOOD. Casualties NIL.	
BECOURT	21		Rodd. Company moved by march route to HENENCOURT. Reinforcements received 20 OR. Casualties NIL.	
HENENCOURT	22		Fine. Sunny. Coy. resting. 3 officers reported for duty (Lt HERBERT and 2/Lts MONTEAGNI and MCLAUGHLIN) Casualties NIL.	
	23		Fine - Sunny.	
	24		Fine. Sunny. Church parade. Casualties Nil.	
	25		Fine. Sunny. Coy. went to bath. Casualties Nil.	
	26		Fine. Sunny. Examination of new draft of 20 OR. Persons reported for duty. Cas. Nil.	
	27		Fine. 1 OR from 7th Bn infantial. Casualties Nil.	
	28		Wet - Fine later. Testing Guns. 1 OR from 8th Bn infantial. Cas. Nil.	
	29		Wet. Coy. moved by march route to ALBERT. Coy. in reserve. Casualties Nil.	
	30		Fine. Coy. resting in reserve. Casualties Nil.	

[signature]
OC 140 M.G. Coy

WAR DIARY
or
INTELLIGENCE SUMMARY

Army Form C. 2118.

VOL 10

1/40th Machine Gun Company.

Place	Date	Hour	Summary of Events and Information	Remarks and references to Appendices
	October 1916			
	1.		Line – 1/40 th Machine Gun Company moved by march route from ALBERT to S. edge of MAMETZ WOOD – Casualties Nil	
	2.		Showery. 1 O.R. reinforcement arrived from base, 1 O.R. attached from 1/5 Batt. London Regt. – Casualties Nil	
	3.		Wet morning, fine later. Lt. G.A.N. WOODCOCK joined Coy. Appointed O.C. – Casualties Nil	
	4.		Wet dull – 1/40 M.G. Coy. relieved 141 M.G. Coy. in line. Coy. H.Q. in BLACKWATCH trench on edge of HIGH WOOD. 8 guns in front line system near EAUCOURT L'ABBE ; 8 guns in support at the COUGHDROP – Casualties Nil.	
	5.		Wet morning, fine later ; 1 O.R. wounded.	
	6.		Fine, warmer, cloudy. H.Q. moved to FLERS SWITCH LINE. Lt. WOODCOCK joined H.Q. and Lt. HARRIOTT returned to transport lines – Casualties Nil.	
	7.		Fine, strong wind. Attack # by 1/40 Infantry Brigade. In afternoon 4 guns moved from COUGH DROP to FLERS SWITCH LINE. Battery guns in FLERS SWITCH line in action during attack. – Casualties Nil.	
	8.		Very wet – 8 guns were found to front line – 1 O.R. wounded, 1 O.R. wounded at duty.	
	9.		Fine – Relief orders received. Coy. relieved by an M.G. Coy. of 9th Divn. – Casualties Nil.	
	10.		Fine – Coy moved to ALBERT. 4 O.R. reinforcements arrived – Casualties Nil.	
	11.		Fine – Limbers cleaned and packed. Belts filled. – Casualties Nil.	
	12.		Fine – Brigade inspected by G.O.C. III Corps. – Casualties Nil.	
	13.		Fine – Entrained at ALBERT station. Transport moved by road to ARGOEUVES. – Casualties Nil	
	14.		Fine – Coy. detrained at LONGPRÉ and moved by march route to VAUCHELLES-LES-DOMART. Transport moved to VAUCHELLES-LES-DOMART by road. – Casualties Nil	
	15.		Showery. Lt. D.L. MCSWEENY proceeded to M.G. training centre, Grantham.	
	16.		Fine – At 12.30 a.m. Coy. moved by march route to LONGPRÉ and entrained. Transport moved to LONGPRÉ and entrained. Coy detrained at CAESTRE (NORD) 2.30 pm. and marched via BOESCHEPE to funkia (near ABEELE) – Casualties Nil	
	17.		Dull – after difference of opinion with various units about billets, Coy moved to another camp ½ mile N.E. – Casualties Nil.	
	18.		Wet – O.C. reconnoitred line and Transport officer reconnoitred Transport lines in forward area. – Casualties Nil.	
	19.		Wet – 1/40 M.G. Coy. relieved 4 Australian M.G. Coy. in BLUFF sector S. of YPRES. 2 guns in reserve, 2 guns in front line, 10 guns in front line system, 2 guns in indirect fire positions, 4 at Burn. on right flank, 142 Brigade on left flank	
	20.		Fine frosty – O.C. reconnoitred line – Casualties Nil.	

Army Form C. 2118.

WAR DIARY
or
INTELLIGENCE SUMMARY

(Erase heading not required.)

140th Machine Gun Company.

Place	Date	Hour	Summary of Events and Information	Remarks and references to Appendices
	October 1916			
	21.		Fine, frosty - 2nd Lt. S.D. CARSON (appt. 2nd in Command) and 10R arrived. - Casualties nil.	
	22.		Fine frosty - Enemy exploded two mines under right sub sector (held by 6th Batt. London Regt). Aeroplane reconnaissance reported Germans massing for attack on crater. 2 reserve guns moved into support position - Casualties nil	
	23.		Fine, cool. - 1 gun withdrawn from front line into reserve. Reserve gun relieved 1 gun in front line system - Casualties nil	
	24.		Wet - Casualties nil.	
	25.		Wet - 1 gun in indirect fire position relieved gun in front line system. 2 guns in front line system withdrawn into reserve. - Casualties N.L.	
	26.		Wet - 2 reserve guns relieved 2 guns in front line system. 2nd Lt. S.D. CARSON proceeded to M.G. training centre GRANTHAM. 10R. returned to 21 M.G. Coy. - Casualties nil.	
	27.		Wet - Casualties nil	
	28.		Wet - 1 O.R. accidentally wounded.	
	29.		Wet - Coy. relieved by 141 M.G. Coy and moved to billets at SCOTTISH CAMP (G.23.a.7.7. sheet 28 N.W.) Casualties nil.	
	30.		Heavy rain. Court of Inquiry convened to inquire into case of No. 5635 L/Cpl A.WOOKEY, accidentally wounded on 28th. President Lt. R.C. CHEESMAN, Members Lt. N.T. HERBERT and 2nd Lt. T.C. PARSONS - Witnesses 22613 Sgt. E.T. PAYNE and 43931 L/Cpl J.R. COOK. - Casualties nil.	
	31.		Wet - Guns cleaned and equipment overhauled - Casualties nil.	

D.M. Woodroof
Capt.
O.C. 140 M.G. Coy

Confidential

Vol XI

War Diary of

140th Machine Gun Company

from 1st November, 1916 to 30th November, 1916.

H.Q.
40th Infantry Brigade

Herewith Original War Diary of this unit for the Month of November.

Robert H. Drayton ⟨?⟩
O.C. 140 M.G. Coy

Ref. No. MG/257
Date 1.12.16.

Army Form C. 2118.

WAR DIARY
or
INTELLIGENCE SUMMARY

(Erase heading not required.)

140 Machine Gun Company

Instructions regarding War Diaries and Intelligence Summaries are contained in F. S. Regs., Part II. and the Staff Manual respectively. Title Pages will be prepared in manuscript.

Place	Date	Hour	Summary of Events and Information	Remarks and references to Appendices
SCOTTISH CAMP G.23.a.7.7. Map 28 N.W.	Nov 1		Bright, frosty. — Company inspected by O.C. — Casualties Nil.	
	2.		Wet. — At 12.15 am, an officer's hut caught fire and was burned to ground. Fire extinguished at 1.0 am. Brigade was inspected by G.O.C. Second Army; owing to inclement weather a march past only was carried out. — Casualties Nil.	
	3.		Court of Enquiry convened by H.Q. 140 Infantry Brigade investigated cause of outbreak of fire on 2nd Nov. — Casualties Nil.	
	4.		Showery. — Coy. Bathed at HOPOUTRE during Battle (POPERINGHE) — Casualties Nil.	
	5.		Fine, pale. — Medal ribbons presented to recipients by G.O.C. 47th Division. — Casualties Nil.	
	6.		Wet. — O.C. reconnoitred HILL 60 Sector (YPRES). Brigade School formed; 1 Sgt instructor and 10 men attended. — Casualties Nil.	
	7.		Wet. All guns and equipment sent to line in charge of Nos. 1 & 2 m guns. — Casualties Nil.	
	8.		Wet. — 140th Infantry Brigade relieved 142 Infantry Brigade in HILL 60 Sector. 141st Infantry Brigade on right flank, on left of 41st Division. 23rd Division on left flank. 140 M.G. Coy. relieved 142 M.G. Coy. Headquarters and reserve section (4 guns) in railway dug-outs at I.20.d.7.9 (Sheet 28 N.W.). 4 guns in front line; 4 guns in MANOR FARM I.22.b.4.4. 3 guns in similar positions. 6th Batt., London Regt. held front line on 140 Brigade front. — Casualties Nil.	See Appendices I
	9.		Fine. — Wind dangerous. — New dug-outs built near Coy H.Q. — Casualties Nil. Lt. R.H. DRAYTON joined (appointed 2nd i/c)	
	10.		Fine, frosty. — Work on H.Q. dug-outs continued — Casualties Nil. — Wind safe.	
	11.		Fine, frosty. — Wind safe. — Work on H.Q. dug-outs continued. Brigade extended its line to right. 8th Batt. London Regt. took over new front line on right of 6th Batt. — Casualties Nil.	

Army Form C. 2118.

WAR DIARY
or
INTELLIGENCE SUMMARY
(Erase heading not required.)

140 Machine Gun Company

Instructions regarding War Diaries and Intelligence Summaries are contained in F. S. Regs., Part II. and the Staff Manual respectively. Title Pages will be prepared in manuscript.

Place	Date	Hour	Summary of Events and Information	Remarks and references to Appendices
	Nov. 12		Fine, Wind safe. — Casualties Nil.	
	13		Mild, Misty early, Wind dangerous. 4th Batt. relieved 8th Batt. in right sub-sector; 15th Batt. relieved 6th Batt. in left sub-sector. Inter-section relief carried out — Casualties Nil.	
	14		Cold, Wind dangerous. — Casualties Nil	
	15		Frosty, do do do	Dispositions unchanged.
	16		do do do do	
	17		do do do do	
	18		Frosty early, rain later, Wind dangerous. Inter-section relief carried out. 6th Batt. relieved 15th Batt. on left and 8th Batt. relieved 15th Batt. in right sub-sector — Casualties Nil	
	19		Wet, Wind Dangerous. — Casualties Nil.	
	20		Dull, Wind Dangerous — O.C. toured line with G.O.C. 47th Division. New M.G. class formed at Brigade School. 10 men sent and others returned to unit — Casualties Nil	
	21		Misty, Wind Dangerous — Casualties Nil	
	22		Fine, Cool. do do do	
	23		Fine, do do do Inter-section relief carried out. 4th Batt. relieved 8th Batt. in right sub-sector, 15th Batt. rel'd 6th Batt. in left sub-sector — Casualties Nil	
	24		Dull, Wind Dangerous; O.C. proceeded on leave; Lieut. R.H. DRAYTON assumed command — Casualties Nil	
	25		Rain, Wind Dangerous — Casualties Nil	
	26		Fine, Mild, Wind safe, message received 8.35 p.m. — Casualties Nil	
	27		Fine, Mild, Capt. Lieut. N.F. MARRIOTT left to take over command of 74th M.G. Coy. Wind dangerous message received 7.30 p.m. — Casualties Nil.	

Army Form C. 2118.

WAR DIARY
or
INTELLIGENCE SUMMARY
(Erase heading not required.)

140th Machine Gun Company

Place	Date	Hour	Summary of Events and Information	Remarks and references to Appendices
	Nov 28		Very Misty, Wind dangerous. 140 Infantry Brigade relieved by 141 Infantry Brigade. 140 M.G. relieved by 141 M.G. Coy and returned to billets at SCOTTISH CAMP (G.23.a.7.7. Map 28 N.W. — Casualties Nil.	
	29.		Misty, Very Cold. Company cleaned equipment and clothing. Lt. N.H.L. BARNI reported for duty. — Casualties Nil	
	30.		Dull, Very Cold. Guns cleaned and equipment overhauled. — Casualties Nil. Lycae Drill, Box Respirator Drill, Revolver Practice, and Instruction in Mechanism carried out	

Robert Dayhi Lt.
Comdg. 140 Coy M.G.C.

Appendix I (WAR DIARY) 140 Machine Gun Coy November 1916

Position of Vickers Guns in Hill 60 Sector
Map reference French Map ZILLEBEKE 28 NW4 & NE 3 1/10000.

	Map reference	Approx. arc of fire (T.B.)	Nature of Emplacement
Front line system	I.29.c.20.35	70° – 110°	Open emplacements
	I.29.a.70.25	80° – 120°	
	I.29.a.80.30	90° – 130°	
	I.29.a.80.65	95° – 130°	
2nd line	I.28.d.35.80	210° – 240°	Open emplacement
	I.28.b.50.55	60° – 150°	do do
	I.23.c.20.05	130° – 210°	Splinter Proof
3rd line	I.27.b.80.30	Right 200° – 230° Centre 100° – 130° Left 40° – 60°	Whizz-bang proof
	I.28.a.25.80	Right 205° – 220° Centre Up road 115° Left 40° – 65°	do do
	I.22.c.45.20	125° – 160°	do do
	I.22.c.75.25	Front 120° – 130° Right 220° – 250°	Splinter Proof
Reserve	I.20.b.20.10	4 Guns in RAILWAY DUG-OUTS.	

Confidential

Original

War Diary of

140th Machine Gun Company

from 1.12.16 to 31.12.16

Vol 12

Army Form C. 2118.

WAR DIARY or INTELLIGENCE SUMMARY

(Erase heading not required.)

140th Machine Gun Company

Place	Date	Hour	Summary of Events and Information	Remarks and references to Appendices
	September 1916			
	1 to 6		During this period the 140th Machine Gun Company was in reserve billets at SCOTTISH CAMP. G.23.a.7.7. The following training was carried out:- Signal drill, Revolver practice, Box Respirator Drill, M.G. instruction (mechanism, immediate action etc.), Physical training. A large amount of work was also done to improve the billets at SCOTTISH CAMP, and the men were also detailed to their work at G.2.H.C.2.5. were bricked and structures erected. Baths were installed to the company on 1st and 2nd Sept. at HOPOUTRE SIDING (POPERINGHE) half the company being bathed on each day. Weather during this period was mostly fine and frosty, but rain fell on 5th Sept. — Casualties Nil.	Lt. Mitchell 28 N.N.
	7.		Wet – O.C. reconnoitred line, and made arrangements for relief. All guns and gun equipment taken to line in afternoon in charge of No. 1 & 2 – Casualties Nil.	
	8.		Wet, Muddy – 140th Infantry Brigade relieved 142nd Infantry Brigade in CANAL SUB SECTOR (YPRES) 1/4th Batt. R.Regt on right, 1/6th Batt. on Centre, 1/8th Batt. on left, 1/5th Batt in reserve. 141st Brigade on left flank 8 guns in right of 23rd Division, 41st Division on right flank. 140 M.G. Coy relieved 142 M.G. Coy dispersed I.25. b. 9.3. 4 front line guns, 4 in support system, 3 in reserve at Coy. HQ on CANAL BANK	
	9.		Wet – Casualties Nil	
	10.		Wet – Increased artillery activity in afternoon and evening. Some shells dropped in grounds of BEDFORD HOUSE (BRIGADE H.Q.) I.26.a.9.3. – Casualties Nil	
	11.		6am-Hostile - Our first Gas attack at 6.35.am. and enough galleries entered about 0.H.a.90.55. Digging party protected by a covering party of 1 N.C.O., 12 men and 2 Lewis Guns. 505 feet of enemy new gallery and quantity of mining apparatus captured. – 1 O.R. wounded	
	12.13		Wet, snow and rain. – Casualties Nil.	
	14.		Fair - Between 3 & 4 pm a trench mortar bombardment covered by Arl. Artillery carried out on HILL 60 sub-sector. Our trench Mortars set were in selected places. – 4 OR reinforcements arrived. Casualties Nil.	

WAR DIARY or INTELLIGENCE SUMMARY

Army Form C. 2118.

140th Machine Gun Company

Place	Date	Hour	Summary of Events and Information	Remarks and references to Appendices
	December 15		Lieut - O.C. sent to Divisional Rest Station sick. From 9.20 a.m. to 10 a.m. enemy artillery and trench mortars bombarded what is of our front causing considerable damage to our Trenches. Our artillery and trench mortars replied vigorously. At 4.10 pm enemy bombarded left and right BLUFF CRATERS. At 4.30 pm our artillery opened fire on S.O.S. Lines in S.B.S. signal being sent up by 6th Division on left. (23rd) Casualties Nil. At 6 pm a 15 minute bombardment carried out by Heavy and Field Howitzers and trench mortars of BLUFF area at 1 pm and ————— and of HILL 60 at 3.50 pm - Casualties Nil.	
	16.		Misty - Casualties Nil.	
	17. 18.		Four - 1/15th Batt. London Regt. relieved 1/16th Batt. (on Regt. in centre section. 110 M.G. Coy. carried out inter section relief 4 guns on right section of front line system relieved by reserve section left front line system guns relieved by section in support system.	
	19.		Frosty - Gunfight expected under German area opposite Hill 60 at 2 am.	
	20.		Rainy - 1 O.R. Killed	
	21.		Wet - Casualties Nil	
	22.		Wet - A raiding party of 2 officers and 50 O.R. entered enemy trenches at I.34.d.10.45. No prisoners were taken but identifications were brought back. Estimated German casualties 12 killed 10 wounded. Casualties among raiding party 3 wounded. Covering fire was given by 1 gun of M.G. Coy. - Casualties 2 O.R. killed 10.R. wounded. (15th Batt.)	
	23.		Very Windy. Inter-section relief carried out 1/6th Batt. London Regt relieved 1/7th Batt. on right section - Casualties Nil.	
	24.		Fine - 1 Batt. withdrawn from line. 2 remaining Battalions extended to man Brigade front which remained unchanged. Disposition - Right Batt. 1/6th Batt. London Regt.; Left Batt. 1/15th Batt. London Regt.; Support Battalion - 1/16th Batt. London Regt.; Reserve Batt. - 1/7th Batt. London Regt. - Casualties Nil.	
	25.		Fair - Casualties Nil.	
	26.		Dull - 2nd Lt. C.G. McLACHLAN wounded.	
	27.		Frosty - Casualties Nil.	
	28.		Hard Frost - 6th & 15th Batt. relieved by 1/20th & 1/17th Batt. London Regt. respectively. Command of sector taken over by G.O.C. 141st Infantry Brigade at 8 pm - Casualties Nil.	

Army Form C. 2118.

WAR DIARY
INTELLIGENCE SUMMARY

140th Machine Gun Company.

(Erase heading not required.)

Place	Date	Hour	Summary of Events and Information	Remarks and references to Appendices
	December 29		Rain - 7th & 8th Batts. relieved by 18th & 19th Batts. London Regt. respectively - 10R reinforcement arrived - Casualties Nil	
	30.		Wet - 140 T.M. Battery relieved by 141 T.M. Battery. 140th M.G. Coy relieved by 141 M.G. Coy and returned to old billets at SCOTTISH CAMP. - Casualties Nil.	
	31.		Fine - Coy resting in reserve - Casualties Nil.	

R. Heenan Lieut
A/ O.O. 140th COY. M.G. CORPS

Vol 13

<u>Confidential</u>

Original War Diary

of

140th Machine Gun Company

from 1st January, 1917 to 31st January, 1917.

WAR DIARY or INTELLIGENCE SUMMARY

Army Form C. 2118.

140th Machine Gun Company

Place	Date	Hour	Summary of Events and Information	Remarks and references to Appendices
	January 1917			Ref Map Sheet BELGIUM 28 N.W.
	1.		Fair – Company resting in reserve at SCOTTISH CAMP G.23.a.7.9. – Casualties Nil	
	2.		Fair – do – do – do – do – do – Casualties Nil	
	3.		Dull – do – do – do – do – do – MAJOR G.A.N.WOODCOCK returned from hospital – Casualties Nil	
	4.		Dull – Company dinner held – Casualties Nil	
	5.		Fair – Divisional M.G. scheme came into operation; all 3 M.G. Coys of Division manning Divisional front. 140 M.G. Coy (3 sections) proceeded to line; 1 section remained at SCOTTISH CAMP. Gun positions to be manned by 140 M.G. Coy are detailed at end of the month's diary. – Casualties Nil	
	6.		Wet and Dull – H.Q. teams were out at Y.M.C.A. hut SCOTTISH LINES; turned to ground – Casualties Nil	
	7.		Fine early, wet later – Casualties Nil	
	8.		Changeable – 140th Infantry Brigade relieved 142nd Infantry Brigade on HILL 60 Sub-Sector – Casualties Nil	
	9.		Rain, windy – Casualties Nil	
	10.		Fair – Interaction relief carried out – Casualties Nil	
	11.		Snow, fine later – Casualties Nil	
	12.		Shindy – Casualties Nil	
	13.		Rain – Casualties Nil	
	14.		Misty – Casualties Nil	
	15.		Fine early, slight mist later – Interaction relief carried out – Major G.A.N. WOODCOCK to Divl. Rest Station, Command taken over by Lt. R.H DRAYTON – Casualties Nil	
	16.		Dull, frosty – Bombardment of German front line system on Divl. front carried out from 7.15a.m. to 7.30a.m. and 9.30a.m. to 4 p.m. 4 guns of 140 M.G. Coy in conjunction with guns of 141 and 142 M.G. Coys carried out indirect barrage fire in bursts from MAG's DEEP during the bombardment. Casualties Nil	
	17.		Snow – Indirect fire (M.G.) continued during morning. Further bombardment postponed owing to adverse weather conditions – Casualties Nil	

Army Form C. 2118.

140th Machine Gun Company.

WAR DIARY
or
INTELLIGENCE SUMMARY
(Erase heading not required.)

Instructions regarding War Diaries and Intelligence Summaries are contained in F. S. Regs., Part II. and the Staff Manual respectively. Title Pages will be prepared in manuscript.

Place	Date	Hour	Summary of Events and Information	Remarks and references to Appendices
	January 1917 18.		Dull – German artillery activity on front line support in BLUFF sector rather above normal. – Army Commander inspected transport lines of 140 M.G. Coy. – Casualties Nil	
	19.		Dull – Lieut H. TUFFILL (and fatigue) joined Coy. as temporary O.C. – At 11.30 p.m. a raid was carried out by 123rd Infantry Brigade on left sub. sector of N.W. Divl. front (on right of 47th Divn); 2 M.G's of 140 M.G. Coy. fired from MAG'S DEN on German trenches on left flank of raiding party. Our artillery created a diversion by shelling German trenches in front of BLUFF. – Casualties Nil	
	20.		Prophylactic – Intersection relief carried out – Our heavy artillery carried out about S.O.S. between 10 and 11 p.m. – Casualties Nil	
	21.		Frosty, Dull – YPRES shelled intermittently during day. Increased hostile machine gun fire on whole of Divl. front. – Casualties Nil	
	22.		Dull, Frosty – 140th Infantry Brigade carried out inter-battalion relief in HILL 60 sub. sector. – Casualties Nil	
	23.		Fine, hard frost – Bombardment of enemy trenches by Heavy Artillery commenced 9 a.m. 4 M.G's of 140 M.G. Coy. and 2 guns of 141st M.G. Coy. carried out indirect fire on enemy communication trenches from MAG'S DEN. – Enemy aircraft very active over our lines. – Casualties Nil	
	24.		Fine, hard frost – Enemy aeroplane very active; 4 of our machines forced to descend. – Casualties Nil	
	25.		Fine, hard frost – BEDFORD HOUSE and surrounding batteries severely shelled by German "heavies" from 1 p.m. to 3 p.m. – Intersection relief carried out – Casualties 2 O.R. wounded	
	26.		Fine, Frosty – 141st Infantry Brigade relieves 140th Infantry Brigade in CANAL sub-sector – Casualties Nil	
	27.		Fine, Frosty – Casualties Nil	
	28.		Fine, Frosty – LANK HOF FARM, BEDFORD HOUSE and road between these points somewhat heavily shelled. This caused when our counter-batteries retaliated. – Casualties Nil	
	29. 30.		Fine, Frosty – LANK HOF FARM again shelled – Casualties Nil. Dull, Snow – Intersection relief carried out – 10R found from 1/15th Batt. London Regt. – Casualties Nil	

Army Form C. 2118.

WAR DIARY
or
INTELLIGENCE SUMMARY

140th Machine Gun Company

(Erase heading not required.)

Instructions regarding War Diaries and Intelligence Summaries are contained in F. S. Regs., Part II. and the Staff Manual respectively. Title Pages will be prepared in manuscript.

Place	Date	Hour	Summary of Events and Information	Remarks and references to Appendices
	January 1917			
	31		Line Frosty — Casualties Nil	
			Positions of Guns manned by 140th Machine Gun Company —	
			I. 34. c. 62. 42.　　　I. 26. d. 05. 30.	
			I. 33. d. 45. 52.　　　I. 34. c. 20. 20. (two guns)	
			I. 33. d. 48. 50.　　　O. H. a. 15.14. (on 41st Div. front)	
			I. 32. b. 25. 90.	

W. Tuffill. Lieut
O/c 140th Company, M.G.C.

Vol 14

Confidential

Original War Diary

of

140th Machine Gun Company

from 1.2.17   to   28.2.17.

WAR DIARY
INTELLIGENCE SUMMARY

(Erase heading not required.)

Army Form C. 2118.

140th Machine Gun Company.

Place	Date	Hour	Summary of Events and Information	Remarks and references to Appendices
CANAL SUB-SECTOR YPRES.	February 1		Line, frosty; 140th M.G. Coy manning 8 guns as indicated in diary for January, 1917. Enemy artillery active on batteries and stationary system. At 2 p.m. enemy commenced to minenwerfer BLUFF CRATERS but was soon silenced on retaliation. YPRES heavily shelled. Major Woodcock returned from Army Rest Station. Casualties — 1 O.R. killed.	
	2.		Line, frosty; Zeppelin reported passing over DICKEBUSCH Y.30 b. — Casualties Nil.	
	3.		Line, frosty; DICKEBUSCH shelled during morning. 140th Infantry Brigade relieved 142nd Infantry Brigade in CANAL sub-sector. — Casualties Nil.	
	4.		Line, frosty; Inter-Section relief carried out. Major WOODCOCK is 147th Divl. Rest Station — Casualties Nil.	
	5.		Line, frosty; Artillery activity on both sides much below normal. Hostile Machine Gun and Trench Mortar activity also below normal. Enemy aircraft active — Casualties Nil.	
	6.		Line, frosty; Hostile artillery fairly quiet on Divl. front. Aircraft day active on Divl. front. Hostile artillery very active on 23rd Divn. (i.e. Left Divn.) front — Casualties Nil.	
	7.		Line, frosty; Hostile artillery very quiet but some minenwerfer activity. Inter-Battalion relief carried out in left sub-section. CANAL Sub-sector. — Casualties Nil.	
	8.		Line, frosty; Front line system and Back Area shelled slightly. 41st Divn. (right) carried out two raids during night — Casualties Nil.	
	9.		Line, frosty; Inter-team relief carried out. 1 team of each section now in reserve at SCOTTISH CAMP. G.23.a.7.7. — Casualties Nil.	
	10.		Line, frosty; WOODCOTE HOUSE and vicinity heavily shelled during morning — Casualties Nil.	
	11.		Line, frosty; 142nd Infantry Brigade relieved 140th Infantry Brigade in HILL 60 Sub-sector — Casualties Nil.	
	12.		Line, frosty; Our artillery demonstrated during night on Left Division front. — Casualties Nil.	
	13.		Line, slight thaw, fog again in evening; BEDFORD HOUSE and vicinity shelled intermittently from 1 p.m. till dusk. Our artillery demonstrated during night on 23rd (Left) Division front. — Casualties Nil.	
	14.		Line, Cold; Inter-team relief carried out. Hostile artillery above normal on back area — also aeroplane activity. — Casualties Nil.	

Army Form C. 2118.

140th Machine Gun Company

WAR DIARY
INTELLIGENCE SUMMARY
(Erase heading not required.)

Instructions regarding War Diaries and Intelligence Summaries are contained in F.S. Regs., Part II. and the Staff Manual respectively. Title Pages will be prepared in manuscript.

Place	Date	Hour	Summary of Events and Information	Remarks and references to Appendices
Line, Gla - KRUISSTRAAT, YPRES, and CAFÉ BELGE	February 15.		Shelled during day. - Casualties Nil.	(Map Sheet BELGIUM 28 N.W.)
	16.		Fine, early rain later - BEDFORD HOUSE and Coy H.Q. shelled heavily during day - Casualties Nil.	
	17.		Fine, mild; Enemy attempted to raid our trenches at I.34.d.05.40. All party was fired upon, 4 were killed and several were wounded of whom 2 were taken prisoners. - Casualties Nil.	
	18.		Dull, Mild; Staff 2 O.R. joined - Casualties Nil.	
	19.		Dull, Mild; Inter-Coy relief carried out. 140th Infantry Brigade, less Brigade H.Q., 140th Trench Mortar Battery, and 1/6 Battalion, London Regt. relieved by 141st Infantry Brigade. Cutting of knotle were in CANAL Sub-sector continued. Enemy's guns fairly active on front system in afternoon - Casualties Nil.	Note. - Enemy's front and support lines entered.
	20.		Dull, Mild; Raid on enemy's trenches in I.34.N.N.A. carried out by 1/6 Batt. London Regt. Enemy's trenches entered at 5 p.m. and evacuated at 6 p.m. 1 officer, 113 OR. and 5 machine guns captured. Dug-outs and two mine-shafts blown up. 4 guns of 23rd Division & of 1442 M.G. Coy., 5 of 1441 M.G. Coy. of 140th M.G. Coy. co-operated; also 140th Trench Mortar Battery. A dummy raid on HILL 60 Sub-sector was carried out 5 minutes before zero. Enemy's retaliation consisted of shelling BLUFF Craters and putting up flares on our front line from 5 to 6 p.m. Casualties of raiding party very slight. Casualties of 140th Infantry Brigade relieved - Casualties Nil.	
	21.		Mild; Enemy artillery very quiet all day - Our artillery active - Casualties Nil.	
	22.		Dull, Mild; Enemy activity Nil. Our artillery active. - Casualties Nil.	
	23.		Misty; Enemy activity nil. Our artillery active. 2nd Lt. A.E. FIFE and 3 OR. joined. - Casualties Nil.	
	24.		Dull; Raid carried out on 41st Divl. front. 1 officer & 54 OR. captured. BEDFORD HOUSE and vicinity heavily shelled in retaliation. Inter-team relief carried out. - Casualties Nil.	
	25.		Fine; Hostile artillery slightly more active on front and Communication trenches. - Casualties Nil.	
	26.		Fine; Casualties Nil.	
	27.		Dull; 140th Infantry Brigade relieved 1442 Infantry Brigade in HILL 60 Sub-Sector. - Casualties Nil.	
	28.		Dull, Misty; Staff 4 OR. joined. - Casualties Nil.	

2449 Wt. W14957/M90 750,000 1/16 J.B.C. & A. Forms/C.2118/12.

Vol 15

Confidential.

Original War Diary

of

140th Machine Gun Company

from

1st to 31st March, 1917.

Army Form C. 2118.

Instructions regarding War Diaries and Intelligence Summaries are contained in F.S. Regs., Part II. and the Staff Manual respectively. Title Pages will be prepared in manuscript.

WAR DIARY
or
INTELLIGENCE SUMMARY

(Erase heading not required.)

140th Machine Gun Company

Place	Date 1917	Hour	Summary of Events and Information	Remarks and references to Appendices
"Foret"	March 1		140th M.G. Coy. still holding positions in CANAL Sub-sector, together with 141st M.G. Coy. Positions of guns defended. Heavy hostile shelling of front system, battery positions and back area. Sub-sector relief carried out. — Casualties Nil.	Ref. Map BELGIUM 28 NW. Table showing dispositions of M.G's in CANAL SUB- "SECTOR" attached.
	2.		Dull — Enemy again shelled back area. Suspected hostile relief dealt with by artillery and M.G. fire. — Casualties Nil	
	3.		Frosty early, dull, misty. — Casualties Nil	
	4.		Bright — Aeroplanes active on both sides. Hostile artillery fairly active. Retaliatory shells employed in our case. 1 aeroplane brought down in I.28.d. Zeppelin reported passing over Kemmel 9.0 p.m. — Casualties Nil.	
	5.		Snow — Artillery very quiet. — Casualties Nil.	
	6.		Bright — Hostile aeroplanes active. Inter-section relief carried out. — Casualties Nil.	
	7.		Dull, cold east wind. — YPRES SQUARE and RAVINE shelled. 142nd Infantry Brigade relieved 141st Infantry Brigade in CANAL Sub-sector. — Casualties Nil.	
	8.		Cold, windy, snow. — A Coy. proceeded to STEENVOORDE for 2 days' Tactical training in Machine Guns. Hostile artillery quiet in forward area but active on Chateau SEGARD, LANKHOF FARM, and DICKEBUSCH LAKE. At 8.20 p.m. enemy blew a small mine at I.29.c.y.13. No damage to our trenches and galleries and no action followed. Enemy's front line slightly damaged. Crater 30 yards from our front line. — Casualties Nil.	
	9.		Cold, some snow. Intermittent shelling of BLUFF and THAMES STREET during morning. — Casualties Nil	
	10.		Dull, mild. Artillery quiet. 1 OR. evacuated. 1 OR. to UK for admission to Cadet unit. — Casualties Nil.	
	11.		Dull, mild. — Hostile artillery very quiet in CANAL Sub-sector but very active on CHATEAU BELGE, CAFÉ BELGE, and CHATEAU SEGARD. Enemy's aeroplane activity in morning. 2 OR. evacuated. Inter-section relief carried out. — Casualties Nil.	
	12.		Rainy. — O.C. (Lt TUFFILL) returned. — Casualties Nil.	
	13.		Changeable. — JACKSON'S DUMP, MANOR FARM, WOODCOTE HOUSE, and back area generally slightly shelled — Dull, 1 OR. arrived. — Casualties Nil.	

WAR DIARY or INTELLIGENCE SUMMARY

Army Form C. 2118.

Place: 140th Machine Gun Company

Date	Hour	Summary of Events and Information	Remarks and references to Appendices
March 14th 1917		Rainy. — Enemy shelled YPRES and roads. Raid attempted by right (141st) Division but failed owing to violent hostile trench mortar barrage on our wire. — Casualties Nil.	
15.		Fair. — 141st Infantry Brigade relieved 140th Infantry Brigade on HILL 60 Sub-Sector. 2 German aeroplanes brought down. — Casualties Nil.	
16.		Fair. — Artillery quiet. Intensive relief carried out. — Casualties Nil.	
17.		Fine. — YPRES shelled heavily. Fairly quiet on front. — Casualties Nil.	
18.		Fine generally, somewhat cloudy. — Hostile artillery unusually active; apparently registering on roads and railways in back area. — Casualties Nil.	
19.		Fine, windy, rain later. — Quiet generally. YPRES shelled. At 5.40 pm. enemy blew in camouflet in front of BLUFF about 100 feet east of "C" crater. Slight damage caused to our gallery. — Casualties Nil.	
20.		Windy, rain. — Enemy shelled our front and support trenches. — Casualties Nil.	
21.		Fair. — At 12.46 a.m. Enemy exploded small mine at I.29.c.75.15. Our trenches slightly damaged. BEDFORD HOUSE heavily shelled (11 a.m. several enemy line considerably damaged. No action followed. Enemy snipers unusually active. 140th Infantry gaps cut in enemy wire North of Canal. 141st Infantry Brigade in CANAL Sub-Sector. Later Sector relieved carried out. — Brigade relieved 140th Infantry Brigade in CANAL Sub-Sector. Later Sector relieved out. — Casualties Nil.	
22.		Changeable; sunshine, hail, snow. — BRISBANE DUMP shelled in morning. Artillery (hostile) active all day and well into night. Burful fire on DICKEBUSCH and CAFÉ BELGE in afternoon. — Casualties Nil.	
23.		Fine. — Hostile artillery activity about normal on front line, battery positions, and back area. — Casualties Nil.	
24.		Fine. — Hostile biplane brought down at 9.15 a.m. at I.34.d.43.62. and destroyed by artillery fire. Enemy artillery and minenwerfer very active all day, especially from 5 pm to 7 pm. At 7.30 pm. enemy raided our line in front of BLUFF and on left front of right (141st) Division, at the same	

WAR DIARY
or
INTELLIGENCE SUMMARY

(Erase heading not required.)

Army Form C. 2118.

140th Machine Gun Company

Place	Date 1917	Hour	Summary of Events and Information	Remarks and references to Appendices
	March 24th (cont'd)		Mine exploding a small mine in Hill 60 hut sector. The Germans entered "A" (Bluff) crater but were driven out later. Our trenches and dugouts were seriously damaged. LIEUT. R.H. GODDARD joined. — Casualties Nil.	
	25.		Snow at intervals, cold. Artillery very active all day and up to a late hour in evening, principally on back areas. Several days shooting since last summer. At night 40 or 50 Germans were seen approaching our trenches, but were dispersed before reaching our wire by Lewis Gun and artillery fire. — Casualties Nil.	
	26		Wet. Heavy artillery generally quiet. Some shelling of back areas. JACKSON'S DUMP shelled 10 p.m. Interaction relief carried out. B Section going to SCOTTISH CAMP. Casualties Nil.	
	27		Dull, cold, windy. Hostile artillery mainly directed on battery positions or back areas. Bombardment of German trenches in I.34.d by Heavy and Field Howitzers from 4.5.30 p.m. Enemy did not reply on front system but shell back areas from 6 to 8 p.m. Enemy threw up small camouflet at about I.29.c.70.05 at 11.30 p.m. causing no trouble MG activity during the night in the neighbourhood of the BLUFF — Casualties Nil.	
	28		Fine. Enemy artillery fairly active all day especially in back areas. LANKHOF FARM heavily shelled in afternoon — Casualties Nil.	
	29		Wet. Artillery fairly quiet — Casualties Nil.	
	30		Fine. Heavy artillery fairly quiet – Casualties Nil	
	31		Bright, cold, occasional showers. Artillery fairly quiet. Back area slightly shelled in morning — Casualties Nil.	

Robert Drayton Lieut
for O.C. 140th COY. M.G. CORPS.

Vol 16

Confidential

Original War Diary

of

140th Machine Gun Company

from

1st April, 1917 to 30th April, 1917.

140th Infantry Brigade.

Herewith Original War Diary
for month of April, 1917.

H. Tuffill. Capt
O.C. 140 M.G. Coy

[Stamp: 149 Machine Gun Company. Ref. No. MG/2444 Date 3/5/17]

Army Form C. 2118.

WAR DIARY
INTELLIGENCE SUMMARY
(Erase heading not required.)

140th Machine Gun Company

Instructions regarding War Diaries and Intelligence Summaries are contained in F. S. Regs., Part II. and the Staff Manual respectively. Title Pages will be prepared in manuscript.

Place	Date 1917	Hour	Summary of Events and Information	Remarks and references to Appendices
April	1		Line. – Increased activity of hostile artillery, mainly on back areas. 12.30 pm to 1.5 pm the CAFE BELGE – DICKEBUSCH road was shelled by 15 cm howitzer. This locality was also shelled between 4 pm and 5 pm. 140th M.G. Coy. still holding CANAL sub-sector in conjunction with 141 H.G. Boy. – Casualties Nil.	Map Sheet Belgium 28 N.W. 28 S.W. 1/20,000
	2		Dull, cold weather – Hostile artillery fairly active on front line and a few shells on back area. Hostile aerial reconnaissance of our lines in morning. 4 pm to 5.30 pm howitzer bombardment of Hill 60 carried out – Casualties 1 O.R. wounded	
	3		Cold, overcast, calm and sunny later. Hostile artillery fairly quiet. Hostile aircraft active during afternoon. Casualties Nil.	
	4		Line. Hostile artillery almost inactive. Cutting of German wire in I.34.b.+d. continued. Our artillery and minenwerfer retaliation on our front system. At 10.15 p.m. we exploded a charge in front of BLUFF CRATERS, the enemy having attempted to break into one of our galleries from the surface in the CANAL BANK – Casualties Nil.	
	5		Line – 3.30 a.m. a working party (enemy) at I.34.d.04.27. dispersed by our artillery. Enemy artillery fairly active on back area. Retaliation for our wire cutting again fairly heavy. Our bombardment has caused considerable damage to enemy's trenches. At 11.45 p.m. a bombing party of Germans endeavoured to surprise Lewis Gun on right of HEDGE ROW, but were driven off having several stick and spherical bombs behind. Inter-sector relief carried out 2 O.R. to H.Q. for Commission, 1 O.R. transferred to Railway Unit – Casualties Nil.	
	6		Line – At 12.15 a.m. another working party at I.34.d.04.04 dispersed by our artillery. Intermittent hostile shelling of trenches and back area all day, and hostile aircraft fairly active in morning. 1 Pl/Sgt., London Regt. relieved 2 Bn/Batt., London Regt. on left sub section – Casualties Nil.	

Army Form C. 2118.

WAR DIARY
—or—
INTELLIGENCE SUMMARY
(Erase heading not required.)

140th Machine Gun Company.

Instructions regarding War Diaries and Intelligence Summaries are contained in F.S. Regs., Part II. and the Staff Manual respectively. Title Pages will be prepared in manuscript.

Place	Date 1917	Hour	Summary of Events and Information	Remarks and references to Appendices
April	7		Overcast. — In convoy 18th Batt. carried out raid on German trenches on I. 3H. 6 and d. 19. Prisoners were taken and many dead were discovered in German trenches. 2 emplacements and 8 dug-outs were destroyed. Enemy barraged his own and our front line rendering withdrawal difficult. 4 M.G.'s of 39th Division; H.Q. of 1 & 2 M.G. Coys, 5 of 141 M.G. Coy, 7 of 140 M.G. Coy co-operated. 15th Batt. London Regt. relieved 18th Batt. London Regt. in left sector. At 11.45 pm. a hostile plane dropped down over 47th Div. H.Q. (HOOGRAAF) and fired on a motor convoy with machine gun, subsequently dropping several bombs. 1 man was killed and 2 wounded. — Draft of 3 O.R. joined, and 1 O.R. rejoined from Base. — Casualties 2 O.R. wounded.	
	8.		Fine. — Hostile artillery active in back areas, especially on KANKHOF FARM and BEDFORD HOUSE. Hostile aircraft also active in morning. Our aeroplanes were fired at with rifles and machine guns from German trenches. — Casualties Nil.	
	9.		Snowy fair intervals. — 23rd Division appears in between 39th & 47th Divisions taking over Hill 60 left sector. The 47th Division moved slightly to right, the 7th Batt. London Regt. taking over line to immediate right of CANAL from 11th Batt. Royal West Kent Regt. (41st Division) Enemy bombarded trenches opposite HILL 60 strong point of 23rd Div. front from 12 noon till 6.40 pm, when he tried to raid along whole front; he was immediately ejected leaving several dead and 1 wounded prisoner. Enemy put up shell barrage on entering our trenches at two points. — Casualties Nil.	
	10.		Low fair intervals, strong wind. — Hostile artillery very quiet. Enemy reported trenches in DICKEBUSCH – KRUISSTRAAT road, especially near BRISBANE DUMP, — from 6.30 – 8.30 pm. — Casualties Nil.	

Army Form C. 2118.

140th Machine Gun Company.

WAR DIARY
or
INTELLIGENCE SUMMARY

(Erase heading not required.)

Instructions regarding War Diaries and Intelligence Summaries are contained in F. S. Regs., Part II. and the Staff Manual respectively. Title Pages will be prepared in manuscript.

Place	Date 1917	Hour	Summary of Events and Information	Remarks and references to Appendices
April	11.		Dull, snow & rain. YPRES SALIENT. Hostile artillery generally very quiet. 140 M.G. Coy. took over 6 guns from 122 M.G. Coy. in SPOIL BANK Section, 1 in GULL SUBWAY, 1 in MELVILLE STREET, and LB 10, 11, 12, and 12P. Our reserve section took over bed & guns leaving rome in reserve. 1 OR transferred to 47th Divl. Signal Coy. — Casualties Nil.	
	12.		Dull. — Hostile artillery quiet. 142nd Infantry Brigade relieved 140th Infantry Brigade on new Divl. front (SPOIL BANK Sub Sect.) — Casualties Nil.	
	14.		Bright. — 4 am. a small party of enemy threw bombs into our trenches at about I.34.d.21.71. No damage done. We retaliated with bombs and M.G. fire on retreating Germans. 4.45 to 8.50 pm enemy fired 250 rounds in vicinity of SHRAPNEL CORNER, WOODCOTE HOUSE and surrounding distance also received attention. 1 gun and 2 gun pits being hit. 10.10 p.m. after shelling with Trench Mortars and Field Guns, about 20 Germans appeared over ridge at left of "B" Crater's Lewis Gun post. Fire was at once opened by Lewis Guns and Bombers, and enemy spread in an onrushing movement. Enemy threw about 20 bombs and was then driven off by Lewis Gun fire. — Casualties Nil.	
	13.		Bright.— WOODCOTE HOUSE shelled with 100 rounds at 4.30 pm. Enemy guns fired shells which dropped near OUDERDOM, objective probably being an ammunition dump.— Casualties Nil. Rainy. — Hostile artillery fairly quiet. — Casualties Nil.	
	15.		Bright early, rain in late afternoon. — Casualties Nil.	
	16.			
	17.		Rainy. — Intersection relief carried out. — Casualties Nil.	
	18.		Wet. — Draft 6 OR arrived. — Casualties Nil.	

WAR DIARY

INTELLIGENCE SUMMARY

Army Form C. 2118.

(Erase heading not required.)

110th Machine Gun Company.

Instructions regarding War Diaries and Intelligence Summaries are contained in F. S. Regs., Part II. and the Staff Manual respectively. Title Pages will be prepared in manuscript.

Place	Date 1917	Hour	Summary of Events and Information	Remarks and references to Appendices
April	19. 20.		Dull. — BEDFORD HOUSE slightly shelled. — Casualties Nil. Bright — After heavy bombardment, the enemy raided our trenches in ST. ELOI sector. A few of our men are missing. — Casualties Nil.	
	21.		Bright. — At 11.10 p.m. our miners blew up a small camouflet. Immediately afterwards enemy sent up golden rain rocket but no action followed. — Casualties Nil.	
	22.		Bright. — Considerable aeroplane activity. Hostile planes attacked our observation balloon near OUDERDOM in morning forcing observer to descend in parachute. 140th Brigade H.Q. relieved 142nd Brigade H.Q. in SPOIL BANK sub sector. Hostile aero active Y & P forMitten Nil.	
	23.		Bright — Registration carried out on enemy's trench system, were many points and communicating trenches of front line, known Headquarters and dumps. Later section relief carried out. Hostile artillery further more active.	
	24.		Bright. — Bombardment carried out on points registered on yesterday. Hostile artillery considerably more active than on last few days. On night 23/24th inst, BRISBONE DUMP and vicinity shelled. At 3.30 a.m. a party of Germans 80 strong approached our trenches in I.34.d. but were repulsed by bombs and Lewis Gun. Only 6 men reached our lines and were immediately ejected. A later party advanced in file were also dispersed. Enemy 3 dead in no Mans Land — Casualties Nil.	
	25.		Overcast, fair intervals. — Shortly after 4 a.m. about 20-30 Germans attempted to raid ALLEN CRATER (I.29.d.07.60). They were driven back by our bombers and suffered casualties by our machine guns on their return to their lines. We carried out for subsequent 4 hrs on 2118. Odd trenches and tracks were subjected to heavy and continuous bombardment. DICKEBUSCH and CAFÉ BELGE received minor attention. — Casualties Nil.	

WAR DIARY
INTELLIGENCE SUMMARY

(Erase heading not required.)

Army Form C. 2118.

140th Machine Gun Company

Place	Date 1917	Hour	Summary of Events and Information	Remarks and references to Appendices
April	26		Overcast.- Hostile artillery very active in back area. Café Belge and TROIS ROIS received some 2030 rounds. At 9.15 A.M. an enemy patrol again attempted to enter ALLEN CRATER but were immediately driven off.- Casualties Nil.	
	27.		Cloudy.- We carried out registration as on 23rd inst. ENUFF knoll shelled during morning.- Casualties Nil.	
	28.		Fine.- Registration carried out as on 23rd inst. Hostile artillery active against back area. BEDFORD HOUSE and BRISBANE DUMP were chief targets, over 600 shells being fired in these spots. Later, station relief carried out.- Casualties Nil.	
	29.		Bright.- We carried out bombardment as on 24th inst. Hostile artillery quiet but aeroplanes active.- Casualties Nil.	
	30.		Bright.- Bombardment carried out as on 24th inst.- Casualties Nil.	

M. Tuffill CAPT.
O.C. 140th COY. M.G. CORPS.

Confidential

Original

War Diary

of

140th Machine Gun Company

from 1st May, 1917, to 31st May, 1917.

WAR DIARY or INTELLIGENCE SUMMARY

Army Form C. 2118.

Place	Date	Hour	Summary of Events and Information	Remarks and references to Appendices
May	1917 1		Warm, Bright. – 140th Machine Gun Company still manning guns in CANAL cut. sector and SPOIL BANK Sector. Our artillery carried out a Bombardment on DAMSTRASSE with good effect, and much counter-battery work was done with aeroplane observation. Enemy continued bombardment of various points in back area, WOODCOTE HOUSE and TROIS ROIS being chief targets. His artillery was gun happy, barrage at 4 A.M. but about 4.30 P.M. he fired some 50 rounds in area of SPOIL BANK (I.34.a and c sheet 28. N.W.) Hostile Machine Guns active South of CANAL still annoying. – Draft of 3 O.R. arrived. – Casualties Nil.	
	2		Warm. Bright. – Hostile artillery fairly active on back area and on front line and communication trenches south of CANAL. Hostile aircraft active. 140th Machine gun Company relieved by 142nd Machine Gun Company in CANAL cut sector and SPOIL BANK Sector, and returned to DOMINION CAMP EAST (G.2.3 d.9.7. sheet 28. N.W.) — Casualties Nil.	
	3		Warm. Bright. – Company cleaned guns, gun equipment. 1/7th Bath London Regt. relieved 1/6th London Regt. in SPOIL BANK Sector. 1 O.R. to U.K. on replacement. – Casualties Nil.	

CANAL SUB-SECTOR

Disposition of Machine Guns

O.3.b.8.4	(41st Divn. front)	1
I.34.C.1.2	(BLUFF. Gun Subway)	2
I.33.d.6.4.	(Gordon's Post)	2
I.32.b.2.9 }	(LANKHOF FARM.)	1
I.26.d.1.3		1
I.34.C.5.7.	(KING STREET)	1
I.25.b.7.6.	Coy H.Q. (Reserve)	4
	Total 140th Machine Gun Coy	12

I.34.b.6.8.	(GRAND FLEET STREET)	1
I.34.b.3.7.	(PETTICOAT LANE)	1
I.34.a.9.3.	(LOVERS LANE)	1
I.34.b.1.1.	(32 SUPPORT)	1
I.34.b.2.4.	(RAT ALLEY)	1
I.28.d.3.9.	(S.P. 9)	1
I.28.C.5.0.	(S.P. 8)	1
I.26.d.9.6. }		1
I.27.C.6.6. } B LINE		1
I.27.d.3.9. }		1
I.27.b.8.3 }		1
I.25.b.7.6.	Coy H.Q. (RESERVE)	1
	Total 141 Machine Gun Coy	12

Total CANAL SUB-SECTOR   24 guns.

Army Form C. 2118.

WAR DIARY
or
INTELLIGENCE SUMMARY
(Erase heading not required.)

Place	Date 1917	Hour	Summary of Events and Information	Remarks and references to Appendices
May	4		Warm. Bright. —	
	5		Warm. Bright. —	
	6		Cold. Fine. —	
	7		Cold. Fine. — 2 men attached to Company from Batts. of 140th Infantry Brigade for fire control duty. During the period Company carried out training. Backward men were instructed in Rickman exercises and other M.G. work. 32 men were trained as Bombers. Officer training consisted of class Viva Drill. Route Marching and Physical Drill. The Company's limbers were cleared. Casualties Nil.	
	8		Cold. Showery. —	
	9		Fine. Bright. —	
	10		Fine. Warm. — 2 O.R. M.G.C. joined.	
	11		Warm. Cloudy. — Company attended Field Day under X Corps M.G.O. — 1 O.R. evacuated and 1 O.R. transferred to Transportation Troop Depôt. Casualties Nil.	
	12		Hot. — Company prepared for move. — 1 O.R. evacuated. — Casualties Nil.	
	13		Warm. Somewhat Showery. Company moved by march route from Dominion Camp to R.E. near BOESCHEPE. (Sheet 27/A 4000) — Casualties Nil.	
	14		Fine generally some showers. — Company resumed march to WALLON CAPPELL (3 miles W. of HAZEBROUCK) — Casualties Nil.	
	15		Warm. Fine. — Company resumed march to GRAND DIFQUES (Sheet 87/7 Sheet 9 France 27 A.S.E), 5¼ miles W.N.W. of ST. OMER. Casualties Nil.	

Army Form C. 2118.

WAR DIARY
or
INTELLIGENCE SUMMARY

(Erase heading not required.)

Instructions regarding War Diaries and Intelligence Summaries are contained in F. S. Regs., Part II. and the Staff Manual respectively. Title Pages will be prepared in manuscript.

Place	Date 1917	Hour	Summary of Events and Information	Remarks and references to Appendices
Boy	16	—	Fine but overcast. —	
	17		Dull, some rain — 10.R.M.G.C. joined	
	18		Fine. —	
	19		Sunny. —	
	20		Dull. —	
	21		Showery — 32 men attached from Batts of 140th Infantry Brigade as Carrying Party.	
	22		Wet-early, fine later —	
	23		Fine —	
	24		Fine — Inspected by —	
	25		Fine — 1 O.R. to U.K. for Commission	
	26		Fine. — L.T.C.G. WILLIAMS joined 5 O.R. evacuated	
	27		Fine — 1 O.R. to M.G.C. Base Depôt (Buffpoint).	
	28		Fine.	
	29		Fine.	During the period the following training was carried out:— 8 Ranks taken were trained as Sergts. of Corporals some instruction as of Range & Field Sketching, Map Reading. Party attached from Batts was instructed in Elementary M.G. work and given practical or range. The sections were given Revolver instruction & Rhoka Practice on Range 1 and were trained in tactical handling in the Field. Subaltern Pats, mostly, were instructed in use of that and On 28th and 29th the Company took part in Brigade Exercises, practising attack to be carried out on forthcoming operations. The Transport of the unit were also inspected by the O.O. 47th Divtl. Train. General Ruse M.G.
	30		Fine. Transport moved by march route to BUYSSEHFURE (5miles NE of STOMER) — Cavalrica Ind.	
	31		Fine — Company returned to 61st Field by march route to STOMER by train from STOMER to POPERINGHE and by march route to DOMINION EAST CAMP. Transport moved to DOMINION EAST CAMP from BUYSSEHFURE by road. Cavalrica. Ind.	

H. Tuffill.

Confidential.

Original War Diary

of

140th Coy., Machine Gun Corps

for

June 1917.

140th Machine Gun Company

WAR DIARY
or
INTELLIGENCE SUMMARY
(Erase heading not required.)

Army Form C. 2118.

June 1917

O.O. 140th COY. M.G. CORPS.
CAPT

Place	Date	Hour	Summary of Events and Information	Remarks and references to Appendices
DOMINION EAST CAMP	1.6.17		Fine – C section moved into line under orders of S.M.G.O of 47th Division and took up positions L7, L8, L9, and L10 – Casualties Nil.	Map Sheet 28 Belgium
	2.6.17		Fine – Concentrated Bombardment at 12.10am and 2.10 am on an area of 100 yards radius from O.5.8.58.62. All guns and howitzers (Heavy and field) took part. – A, B and D Sections guns and gun equipment sent up at night and left in charge of a guard. – Casualties Nil.	
	3.6.17		Fine – Bombardment as on night ½ carried out at 12.20 am on area I.35.d.4.8. – I.36.c.2.4 – I.36.c.20. Artillery demonstration along whole of Second Army front at 3.0 pm Consisted of 15 mins intense bombardment with heavy guns followed by 20 mins. barrage. Smoke shells were used. MG boys of 147th Divn carried out MG Barrage to accompany Field Artillery barrage. – 10.30 pm German Battalion H.Q. in DAMMSTRASSE shelled between DOME HOUSE and OGC49. – Casualties Nil.	
	4.6.17		Fine – At 10.30 pm German HQ at O.6.a.55 were shelled – Casualties Nil.	
	5.6.17		Fine – 1 Section of 141st M.G. Coy relieved C Section in L7, L8, L9, L10 positions – heat day of 5 days bombardment of STABLES at WHITE CHATEAU with 9.2" and 12" Howitzers – Casualties Nil.	
Coy. HQ at LOCK HOUSE	6.6.17		Fine – A, B and D Sections went into the line at 4.0 am, 4.15 am and 4.30 am respectively. – C section took over positions R1, R6, R8 and R11 at SPOIL BANK under orders of S.M.G.O. At dusk all MG teams except at R1, R6, R8 and R11 withdrew to battle positions. A section in or near QUEENS ALLEY, B and D sections in or near LOCK HOUSE BANK – Casualties Nil.	
	7.6.17		Fine, storm in evening. – 147th Division cooperated in an attack by Second Army against MESSINES – WYTSCHAETE ridge. The Division attacked with 2 Brigades in the line and one in Reserve. Order of Battle from right to left – 123rd Infantry Brigade (High Division), 140th Infantry Brigade (South of CANAL), 142nd Infantry Brigade (North of Canal). The 24th Division was in Corps Reserve. Zero hour was 3.10 am. The 140th Infantry Brigade the 8th London attacked the Life and the 7th London on the right and captured the Blue line. Phase 2 followed at about Zero + 3 hours when the 6th London on the Life and the 15th London on the right attacked and captured the Black line. Your tanks cooperated. 2 sections (B and D) of this Company went forward at about one hour after zero from their assembly place in NORFOLK ST. N & Kenchester	Operation Order No. 9 attached

2449 Wt. W14957/M90 750,000 1/16 J.B.C. & A. Forms/C.2118/12.

Army Form C. 2118.

140 Machine Gun Coy

WAR DIARY or INTELLIGENCE SUMMARY

(Erase heading not required.)

June 1917

Place	Date	Hour	Summary of Events and Information	Remarks and references to Appendices
YPRES, SPOIL BANK SECTOR.	7.6.17 (cont)		Germans were in two lines. B. on the right and D section on the left. Immediately the Blue line was taken there were 2 guns of B Section and 2 of D section to go forward as soon as Black line was taken. The exact positions of guns in the Blue line were known at Regt. HQ. at 7.15 a.m. B Sections guns being at O.H.C.80.90 and O.H.C.50.15. About an hour and a half after the Black line was taken the four guns which were waiting to advance went forward and took up positions in OPAL RESERVE and behind OBLONG RESERVE covering the whole of the Brigade front. At 8.30 a.m. B Section Officer reported Black line taken, Blue line consolidated and 2 guns in OBLONG TRENCH. The exact positions of guns in the Black line were known at Bay A.8 by 11.0 a.m. and were as follows:— B Section in OBLONG TRENCH at O.10.a.70.65 and O.10.B.15.98. D Section in OPAL RESERVE at O.10.d.93.78 and O.5.c.12.05. All guns were got into position without loss. Hostile shelling of the hostile gunned coming out of the entrenchment inevitable. A section remained in reserve and moved to get positions in the British line. C Section cooperated in the Divisional Barrage under the orders of the S.M.G.O. (17th Bde.) This section as Bh.Q. about 300 yards from our front line between ESTAMINET LANE and OLD KENT ROAD opened fire at Zero hour and continued firing for 77 minutes placing a barrage on the CANAL where it turns abruptly south. Unfortunately the line of the enemy barrage fell along the spot chosen for this battery and two of the guns were put out of action. One man being killed and two wounded. At 10 a.m. A Section moved to OAK RESERVE and took up positions. An ammunition... (unclear) ... C Section left barrage positions and went to LOCK GATES. One old one went to Kent up for use but were ammo ... to improve ... with it.
	8.6.17		June — At left hand position of D Section in OPAL RESERVE gun and tripod were knocked out. — 1 team of A Section took up gun of B (that team of which had become casualties) in OBLONG TRENCH at midday. A Section relieved by a Section from LOCK GATES relieved A Section in OAK RESERVE gun and 2 guns of D in OPAL RESERVE and 2 guns of B in OBLONG TRENCH. These 4 guns went back to LOCK GATES.	
	9.6.17			
	10.6.17		Nine — Dispositions unchanged	

140 Machine Gun Coy WAR DIARY June 1917 Army Form C. 2118.

Place	Date	Hour	Summary of Events and Information	Remarks and references to Appendices
	11.6.17		Fine - Dispositions unchanged.	Map Sheet 28 (Belgium)
	12.6.17		Fine, some rain in afternoon and evening - Brigade relieved by 122 Infantry Brigade - Coy. relieved by 122 M/G Coy. and moved to QUEBEC CAMP. - Casualties Nil.	
QUEBEC CAMP	13.6.17		Fine - Coy. rested at QUEBEC CAMP - Casualties Nil.	
	14.6.17			
	15.6.17		Fine - Coy moved by march route to CAESTRE in evening - Casualties Nil.	Map Sheet
	16.6.17		Fine - Coy moved by march route in evening to Chateau at V.19.c.5.8. near EBBLINGHEM - Casualties 27 (France) Nil.	
EBBLINGHEM	17.6.17		Fine - Coy. rested at EBBLINGHEM - Casualties Nil.	
	18.6.17			
	19.6.17			
	20.6.17		Showery, strong wind - Coy. cleaned guns and carried out gun drill - Casualties Nil.	
	21.6.17		Wet very early morning, fine morning and afternoon, heavy storm in evening - Training mechanism and map shop. Casualties Nil.	
	22.6.17		Showery - A and D Sections bathed in forenoon - Coy. did gun drill and mechanism - Casualties Nil.	
	23.6.17		Cloudy, heavy rain - B and C sections bathed - Casualties Nil.	
	24.6.17		Dull, light intervals, cool - A and D bathed - Coy. carried out tactical scheme Casualties Nil.	
	25.6.17		Cool - Divine service - Casualties Nil.	
	26.6.17		Warmer - A and D carried out Field Training - B and C carried on Gun and Mechanism - Casualties Nil	
	27.6.17		Dull - A and D Field Training, B and C Gun Drill and Mechanism - Casualties Nil	
	28.6.17		Warm, heavy rain in evening - Box Respirator Drill - Cleaning limbers & guns - Casualties Nil	
			Showery early, close all day, storm in evening - Coy. moved by march route to METEREN - Coy HQ at X.9.c.70.25 (Farm) - Casualties Nil.	
YPRES (RIDGE WOOD)	29.6.17		Dull - Coy. moved in afternoon to RIDGE WOOD - Transport took over our lines on 19 CLUTTE - RENINGHELST ROAD. - Casualties Nil.	Map Sh. 28 (Belgium)
	30.6.17		Rainy, dull - Ok. reconnoitred lines - Casualties Nil	

Lt Shaw CAPT.
O.C. 140th COY. M.G. CORPS.

SECRET

140th Machine Gun Company Order No. 9.   Copy No 8

2.6.17.

General Idea.

1. (a) The 47th Division will co-operate in an attack by the Second Army against the MESSINES-WYTSCHAETE ridge. The Division will attack with 2 Brigades in the line and 1 in reserve. Order from right to left — 123rd Infantry Brigade. (41st Division). 140th Infantry Brigade (South of CANAL). 142nd Infantry Brigade. (North of CANAL). The 24th Division will be in Corps Reserve.

   (b) Fronts and objectives allotted to 140th Infantry Brigade are shewn on Map A. Successive objectives are shewn in red, blue and black lines. The black line is the final objective of the Division.

   (c) The advance will subsequently be continued at ZERO + 10 hours by troops from Corps reserve against ODYSSEY TRENCH, OLIVE TRENCH and then to OPAL RESERVE about O.5.C.3.3., this objective being known as the green line.

   (d) The attack will be conducted in two phases.
   Phase 1 will include the attack of the Blue line
   Phase 2 "   "   " advance from the Blue line to the Black line and will follow Phase 1 after an interval of 2 hours 55 mins.
   It is expected that the Red line will be taken at ZERO+ 22
   "   "   "   "   "   Blue "   "   "   " " ZERO+ 47
   "   "   "   "   "   Black "   "   "   " " ZERO+ 578

2. Infantry Dispositions

   The 8th and 7th Batts, London Regt, will carry out the attack in Phase 1, the 8th Batt. attacking on the right and the 7th Batt. on the left. The 15th and 6th Batt. London Regt. will carry out the attack in Phase 2, the 15th Batt. attacking on the right and the 6th Batt. on the left.

3. Code for days and hours.
   (a) Referring to Days.
   "Z" day is the day on which operations take place
   One day before "Z" = "Y" day
   Two days   "   "Z" = "X" "
   Three "   "   "Z" = "W" "
   Four   "   "   "Z" = "V" "
   Five   "   "   "Z" = "U" "
   Days before "U" will be referred to as
      Z-6, Z-7, Z-8, etc.
   1 day after "Z" = "A" day
   2 days after "Z" = "B" "
   3 "   "   "Z" = "C" "
   Days after "C" day will be referred to as :-
      Z+4, Z+5, Z+6, etc.

   (b) Referring to hours on "Z" day.
   Zero is the exact time at which operations will commence, and times will be designated in hours and minutes plus or minus from ZERO even if they encroach on "Y" day.

4. Position of the Company on Successive days up to "Z" day and at ZERO – 2 hrs on "Z" day day is given in APPENDIX "A"

5. Action of M.G's at ZERO
   A Section will remain in it's defensive positions.
   B   "   "   "   support the attack on the right.
   D   "   "   "   "   "   "   " " left.
   C   "   "   "   be employed on barrage work under the orders of the S.M.G.O. (47th Divn.) until Zero + 1½ hours when they will be at the disposal of the G.O.C. Brigade.
   The first objective of B and D Sections will be the consolidation of the BLUE LINE. The Sections will not advance before the RED line has been definitely gained and the actual time of the advance will be determined by any lull or gap in the barrage of which full advantage must be taken. The Sections will not advance beyond the RED line until the BLUE line has been taken. As soon as this has been accomplished each section will push up to the neighbourhood of OAK RESERVE

and take up positions with 2 guns with a view to consolidating the BLUE line. The remaining 2 guns of each section will be in readiness to advance to the BLACK line and when this objective has been taken they will push up to the BLACK line in order to help in its consolidation. Attention is drawn to the possibility of troops assembling for a counter attack in RAVINE WOOD and HOLLEBEKE VALLEY. Section Officers of B and D Sections will keep in constant touch with the O.C. of the Batts. attacking on the right and left respectively.

8 Belt Boxes per gun will be carried by each gun team. 4 empty belts will be taken by each gun team and will be carried by being wound round the man's body. These belts will be filled from the bandoliers of any men who have become casualties. Two bombs per man will be carried.

Ammunition Dumps consisting of the remaining 6 belt boxes per gun will be established under the charge of Section Corporals. They will keep in close touch with the guns as they move forward.

<u>Dress</u> Fighting Order. Cardigans will be rolled in waterproof sheets.

6. Frequent reports, including an estimate of the number of casualties must be sent to Coy. H.Q.

7. <u>Battalion Headquarters</u>
On the night Y/Z the H.Q. of the 8th and 7th Batts. will be at NORFOLK BANK.

After the advance the 8th Batt. will establish a forward Command Post at about O.H.C.2.8. and the 7th Batt. at about O.4.a.9.3.

The 15th and 6th Batts. will establish forward Batt. H.Q. as near O.H.C.2.8. as possible, and when the advance goes forward to the BLACK LINE they will establish forward command posts in the neighbourhood of OAK RESERVE.

8. <u>Rations.</u> When proceeding to the line rations for the following day will be taken on the man in addition to the Iron Ration.

For Y and Z day rations will be dumped at LOCK HOUSE. Iron Rations for A day will be dumped at SPOIL BANK. Rations for B day will, if possible, be brought to LOCK HOUSE on Z/A night.

Water Bottles will be taken into the line full and the greatest economy must be exercised in their use. A dump of 50 gallons of water in petrol cans will be maintained at Coy. H.Q. All ration parties must bring down petrol cans with them.

9. (a) All ranks are warned against the possibility of treachery on the part of the enemy, e.g. signs of surrender and the use of the white flag.
(b) All officers will carry compasses.
(c) No orders, diaries, letters or documents other than the specially issued maps of the German defences are to be taken into the trenches.
(d) All captured documents will be sent to Coy. H.Q. as soon as possible.
(e) All slightly wounded men will carry their ammunition and equipment out of action; anyone disobeying this order will be severely punished.

10. Instructions in regard to routes for transport have been issued separately.

Copies 1 to 4. Section Officers A, B, C, D.
     5. 110th Infantry Brigade
     6. S.M.G.O.
     7. C.O.T.G.O.
     8. War Diary
     9. File.

Robert M Drayton
Lieut and Actg. Adjt.

APPENDIX "A"

Section	Position on W/X night	Position on X/Y night	Position on Y/Z night	Position at Zero - 2 hours on Z day
A	1 gun GUN SUBWAY R5 1 " MELVILLE SUBWAY R8 1 " forward end SPOIL BANK R11 1 " QUEENS ALLEY R1	As on W/X night	As on X/Y night	As on Y/Z night
B	LOCK HOUSE and SPOIL BANK.	As on W/X night	As on X/Y night	Point of assembly to be notified later.
C	This section is under the orders of the O.C. S.M.G.C. 47th Division	As on W/X night	As on X/Y night	As on Y/Z night
D	LOCK HOUSE and SPOIL BANK	As on W/X night	As on X/Y night	Point of assembly to be notified later.
Coy. H.Q.	LOCK HOUSE	As on W/X night	As on X/Y night	As on Y/Z night

Note. B & D Sections will be at their respective points of assembly at Zero - 2 hours, Z day and will report to Coy. H.Q. that this has been done at least one hour and a half before Zero. O.C. B & D Sections will be at Batt. H.Q.s of 8th & 7th Batt, London Regt, respectively (ie NORFOLK BANK) until their sections advance.

MAP A

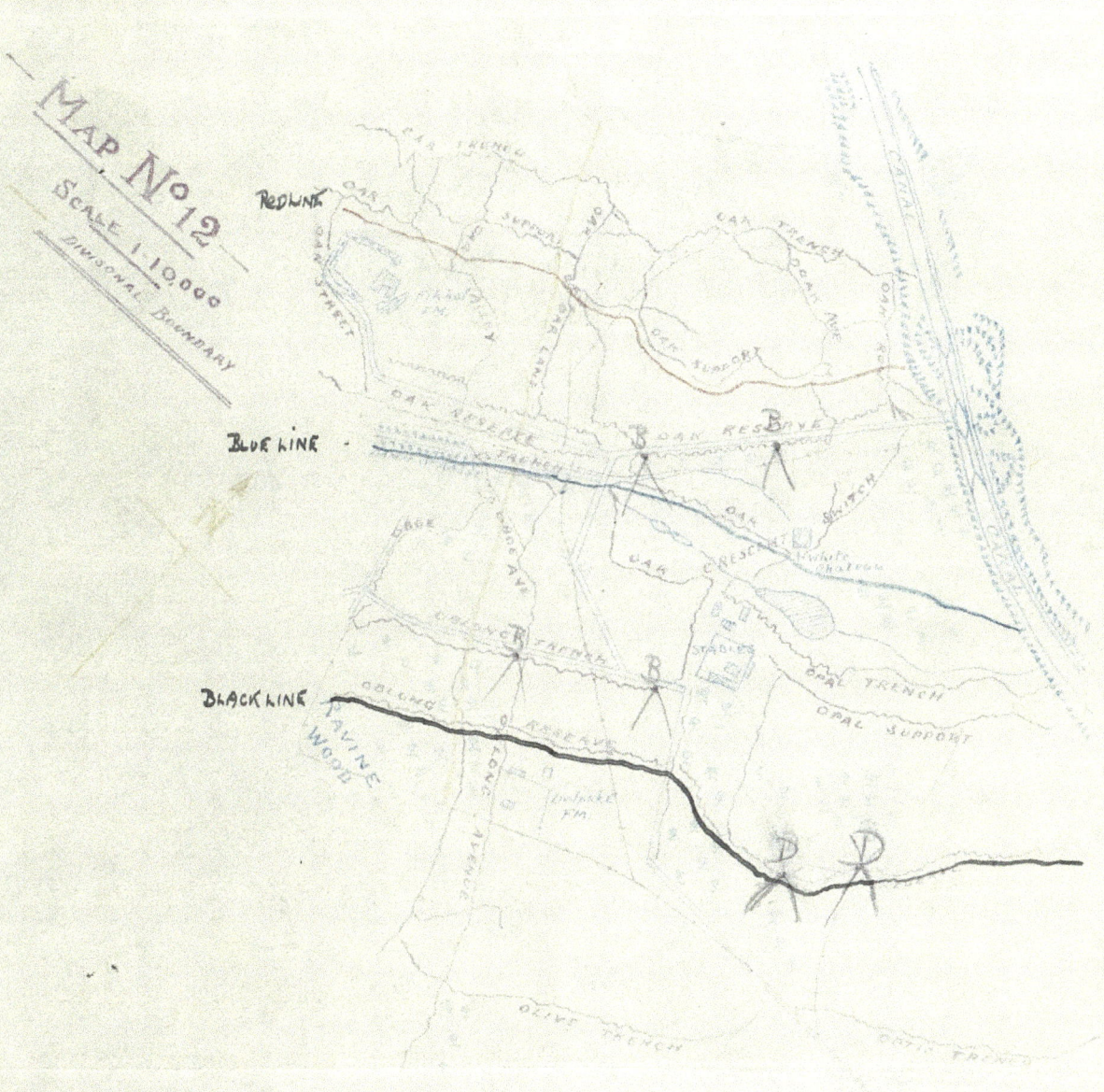

Confidential.
Original
War Diary
of
140th Machine Gun Company
for
July 1917.

Headquarters
140th Infantry Brigade

Herewith Original War Diary of 140 Coy. M.G.C. for July 1917.

T. Parsons
for O.C. 140th COY. M. G. CORPS.

140 Machine Gun Company.
Ref. No. MG/714
Date 1.8.17

Army Form C. 2118.

WAR DIARY
INTELLIGENCE SUMMARY.
(Erase heading not required.)

July 1917

140th Company, Machine Gun Corps — Summary of Events and Information

Place	Date	Hour	Summary of Events and Information	Remarks and references to Appendices
YPRES (SPOIL BANK) (SECTOR)	1.7.17		Dull, cool. — The 140th M.G. Coy. relieved 8 guns of the 142nd M.G. Coy. behind DAMMSTRASSE and 8 guns of the 123rd M.G. Coy. in FRENCH TRENCH (Barrage position). Hostile shelling very active. Enemy doing no work opposite our front. — Casualties Nil.	Coy. H.Q. at SHELLEY DUMP. Ref. Map Sheet 28
	2.7.17		Warm and sunny. — Hostile artillery fairly active. Enemy aeroplanes very active. — 7 O.R. returned from Second Army Rest Camp. 2 O.R. evacuated sick. Casualties Nil.	
	3.7.17		Fine — Enemy shelled WHITE CHATEAU WOOD, SPOIL BANKS and DAMMSTRASSE — Casualties 1 O.R. wounded.	
	4.7.17		Dull, rain. — Coy. relieved. 8 guns relieved by 142 M.G. Coy; 8 guns relieved by 56 M.G. Coy. Coy moved into new billets near RENINGHELST (Coy. H.Q. at G.34.d.9.4. Sheet 28 N.W.) Accommodation very limited. 141 M.G. Coy. already in possession — Hostile artillery very active in morning against our front trench system and tracks — Casualties Nil.	
RENINGHELST	5.7.17		Fine — Coy. resting in Reserve. Guns and gun equipment cleaned — Casualties Nil.	
	6.7.17		Fine — Sections inspected by Section Officers. Ammunition belts cleaned and overhauled. 2 Sections carried out Range firing. Divisional Commander inspected the camp — Casualties Nil.	
	7.7.17		Fine, storm at night — Belt filling carried out in morning. Coy. bathed at WESTOUTRE. 1 O.R. to Base Depot as inefficient — Casualties Nil.	
MURRUMBIDGEE	8.7.17		Dull, rain. — Coy. moved to MURRUMBIDGEE CAMP near LA CLYTTE. Rain prevented Church Parade. 140 Infantry Brigade relieved 142 Brigade South of Canal — Casualties Nil.	
SPOIL BANK SECTOR	9.7.17		Dull, cold — Coy. relieved 142 M.G. Coy. in line South of CANAL. Coy. H.Q. at O.4.c.35.40. — Our artillery carried out trench bombardment. Our fighting patrols under cover of our barrage raided enemy's trenches at night and took eleven prisoners. — Casualties 1 O.R. (transport driver) wounded at duty.	
	10.7.17		Dull, windy. — Enemy artillery active on left of Divisional Front. Lieut. R.G. WHITE (M.G.C.) joined from 88th M.G. Coy. as Second in Command. 1 O.R. evacuated sick — Casualties Nil.	
	11.7.17		Fine — Enemy artillery below normal. Enemy airicraft very active, bringing down four of our balloons. Capt. Donogan returned from leave to U.K. — Casualties Nil.	

Army Form C. 2118.

WAR DIARY
INTELLIGENCE SUMMARY.
(Erase heading not required.)

Instructions regarding War Diaries and Intelligence Summaries are contained in F. S. Regs., Part II. and the Staff Manual respectively. Title pages will be prepared in manuscript.

Place	Date	Hour	Summary of Events and Information	Remarks and references to Appendices
SPOIL BANK SECTOR	12.7.17		140th Bde. Machine Gun Corps — July 1917	Ref. Maps Sheet 28
	12.7.17		Fine — Our front trenches shelled in morning and of NANKHOF FARM later. Enemy aircraft very active — Casualties Nil.	
	13.7.17		Fine — Enemy artillery very active against our forward system — Casualties Nil.	
	14.7.17		Rain early; fine later; storm at night — Heavy shelling of our front and support line — 2 O.R. evacuated sick — Casualties Nil.	
	15.7.17		Fine — Coy. carried out Inter. Section relief — Increased activity of hostile artillery against our back area — Casualties 2 O.R. wounded.	
	16.7.17		Fine — Enemy bombarded I.33 and O.2 with gas shell during night — Casualties Nil.	
	17.7.17		Fine — Enemy artillery was active in the morning and quiet in the afternoon. They shelled our trenches with gas shell at night. 47 Divisional Artillery put a barrage along the Brigade front and the 6th London Regt. followed up the barrage with a patrol directed against OBLIQUE TRENCH and OBLIQUE ROW — Casualties Nil.	
	18.7.17		Rain — Hostile shelling less than usual. Enemy aircraft inactive — Casualties Nil.	
	19.7.17		Rain early, windy, cool — Heavy shelling of BLUFF and SPOIL BANK. 1 O.R. evacuated. Casualties Nil.	
	20.7.17		Fine early, dull later — Exceptionally heavy shelling by enemy during night — Lt. R.G. WHITE (London bombard) to hospital sick — Casualties Nil.	
	21.7.17		Fine — Enemy guns active against our forward areas. Hostile gas shell bombardment during night. Enemy is doing no work opposite our front — Casualties 2 O.R. wounded, 1 O.R. accidentally injured.	
	22.7.17		Fine — Heavy bombardment over the whole of our front area at night. Enemy planes showed great activity over our back areas at night — Casualties Nil.	
	23.7.17		Fine — Heavy barrage on our front and support lines during day. 6th London Regt. carried out successful raid in O.5.d. under cover of a creeping barrage at 10.0 p.m. and captured 29 prisoners. Enemy retaliation consisted of heavy gas shell bombardment — Coy. relieved by 122 M.G. Coy. and Transport moved to camp at M.11.c.3.8. — Casualties 7 O.R. admitted to hospital suffering from the effects of gas from gas shells.	

(A7293). Wt. W12859/M1293 75,000. 1/17. D.D. & L., Ltd. Forms/C.2118/4.

WAR DIARY
INTELLIGENCE SUMMARY.
(Erase heading not required.)

Army Form C. 2118.

July 1917

Place	Date	Hour	Summary of Events and Information	Remarks and references to Appendices
LION CAMP	24.7.17		Fine. - Coy. and Transport Lines moved to LION CAMP (M.11.a.21.) - 140 Infantry Brigade relieved by 122 Brigade. - 7 O.R. evacuated (gas poisoning). - Casualties Nil.	Ref. Map Sheet 28.
	25.7.17		Heavy rain till 1 p.m. Fine and warm later. - Limber equipment cleaned and checked, limbers packed and cleaned. - Casualties Nil.	
	26.7.17		Fine. - 8 O.R. inspected Company Lewis Transport - Casualties Nil.	
	27.7.17		Fine - Limber cleaned. Marking of man's equipment carried out morning. Company bathed at CHIPPEWA in afternoon. 8 O. inspected Transport at 2.30 p.m. Hostile aeroplane dropped bombs in neighbourhood between 10 p.m. and 11 p.m. - Same this Nil. - 2 O.R. evacuated sick.	
	28.7.17		Fine. - Divisional Commander presented Medal Ribbons. Coy. paraded with 15th Batt. London Regt. for this purpose. 2 O.R. of this Coy. among recipients. - 2 O.R. to U.K. for admission to Cadet Unit. Casualties Nil.	
	29.7.17		Rain. - Church Parade cancelled owing to rain. - Casualties Nil.	
	30.7.17		Dull, rain. - 2 O.R. to Second Army Rest Camp - Casualties Nil.	
	31.7.17		Dull, rain. - Attack by Second and Fifth Armies. From 6 a.m. units of 140 Infantry Brigade under orders to move at one hour's notice. 8 men from each of 6th, 7th, 8th and 15th Bns. London Regt. joined Coy. as carrying party. 141st Division took HOCHEBEKE and FORRET FARM after being held up. At 7.30 p.m. orders received that units need no longer remain at one hour notice. Casualties Nil.	

Rearmby [signature] CAPT.
O.C. 140th COY. M.G. CORPS.

[Stamp: 140 Machine Gun Company. Ref. No. MG/7/4. Date: 1/8/17]

Vol 20

Confidential.
Original War Diary
of
140th Company, Machine Gun Corps
for
August 1917.

Army Form C. 2118.

WAR DIARY
or
INTELLIGENCE SUMMARY.
(Erase heading not required.)

140 Machine Gun Company.
Ref. No. M.7/57
Date 2-9-17

140th Company, Machine Gun Corps.
August 1917

Place	Date	Hour	Summary of Events and Information	Remarks and references to Appendices
LION CAMP SHEET 28 SW. M.11.a.2.1.	1.8.17		Rain; 140th Coy. M.G.C. intents and bivouacs at LION CAMP. - Casualties Nil.	
	2.8.17		Rain; 2 OR joined from Base Depot. Casualties Nil.	
	3.8.17		Rain; Casualties Nil.	
	4.8.17		Rain; Company bathed at CHIPPEWA CAMP. - Casualties Nil.	
	5.8.17		Fine at intervals. - Parade Service at CARNARVON CAMP. - 3 OR evacuated. - Casualties Nil.	
	6.8.17		Misty in morning, fine later. - Casualties Nil.	
	7.8.17		Dull. - 2 Lt. N.C. CLIFFORD (M.G.C.) transferred to 12th Coy. M.G.C. - Casualties Nil.	
RIDGE WOOD	8.8.17		Fine early, heavy rain in evening. - Coy. relieved 141 Coy. M.G.C. in RIDGE WOOD. Coy. HQ. at N.5, a.9.4. (Sheet 28 SW) - Casualties Nil.	
	9.8.17		Fair. - E.A. bombed RIDGE WOOD during night. - Casualties Nil.	
	10.8.17		Fine. - 4 OR joined from A.H.T.D. ABBEVILLE. Carrying Party of 6 men of each of 6th, 7th and 8th Batts. LONDON REGT. returned to their units. - Casualties Nil.	
	11.8.17		Fine, storm in evening. - 2 OR rejoined from Base Depot. - Casualties Nil.	
	12.8.17		Showery. - Coy. relieved by 11b Coy. M.G.C. in RIDGE WOOD and moved to ASCOT CAMP. Coy. HQ at M.8 d.8.2. (Sheet 28 SW) - Casualties Nil.	
ASCOT CAMP	13.8.17		Sharp gale. - Sections inspected by Section Officers. Limbers packed and cleaned. 10 OR evacuated. Casualties Nil.	
	14.8.17		Fair; warm. - Company route marched in morning. Sections inspected by Section Officers in afternoon. Coy. bathed at WESTOUTRE BATHS. 1 OR rejoined. - Casualties Nil.	
	15.8.17		Fine. - Coy moved by train from ABEELE to ST. OMER and marched to new billets at ETREHEM. Sheet 27A, S.E. W.10.d. - Casualties Nil.	
ETREHEM	16.8.17		Fine. - Guns and equipment cleaned. - Limbers cleaned and packed. 1 OR rejoined. 17 OR joined from Base Depot. Carrying party of 6 OR returned to 15th Batt. LONDON REGT. - Casualties Nil.	
	17.8.17		Fine. - Coy. carried out elementary tactical handling of guns in the field and physical training. Classes formed for un-gotaken and for instructing Officers and NCO's in same spheres. Casualties Nil.	

Richard Bradley CAPT.
O.C. 140th COY. M.G. CORPS.

Army Form C. 2118.

WAR DIARY or INTELLIGENCE SUMMARY

(Erase heading not required.)

140th Company, Machine Gun Corps

August 1917

140 Machine Gun Company.
Ref No MG/57
Date 2.9.17

Instructions regarding War Diaries and Intelligence Summaries are contained in F.S. Regs., Part II. and the Staff Manual respectively. Title pages will be prepared in manuscript.

Place	Date	Hour	Summary of Events and Information	Remarks and references to Appendices
ETREHEM	18.8.17		Fine — Training carried out as for 17.8.17. Coy bathed at ST. OMER — Casualties Nil.	
	19.8.17		Fine — No parade service owing to men starting long crawl by competing parade at battn.	
	20.8.17		2 Officers went by motor bus to BOULOGNE. 14 O.R. went by bus to ST. OMER afterwards attending a performance by Divl. Concert Party at LONGUENESSE. 1 O.R. to Base Depot as inefficient. Casualties Nil.	
	21.8.17		Fine — Coy carried out elementary tactical handling of guns in the field and physical training. Remaining class paraded. 1 O.R. rejoined from hospital — Casualties Nil.	
ST MARTIN AU LAERT	22.8.17		Fine — Coy moved to new huts at MOULIN A VAPEUR (Sheet 27ASE R 32.b.6.9) near ST. MARTIN AU LAERT — Casualties Nil.	
	23.8.17		Fine — GOC Second Army inspected the Brigade at LONGUENESSE made oration of its leaving the Second Army. — EA dropped bombs near ST. OMER at about 10 p.m. — Casualties Nil.	
	24.8.17		Fine — Coy carried out tactical handling of guns. 1 O.R. rejoined from hospital — Casualties Nil.	
			Fine — Coy moved by bus to VANCOUVER CAMP. Coy HQ at H.14.C.24 (Sheet 28 NW) 1 O.R. rejoined from hospital. 1 Sgt. to MGC Base Depot for passing as instructor. 1 Sgt. to GHQ Small Arms School as Instructor — Casualties Nil.	
VANCOUVER CAMP	25.8.17		Fine — Limbers and equipment cleaned. Limbers packed. Mules surrounded by a standing wall 3 feet high. 1 O.R. evacuated — Casualties Nil.	
	26.8.17		Fine early, rain in evening — Parade service in VANCOUVER THEATRE. O.C., 2nd I/C and 2 Section Officers reconnoitred line. Lieut. R.H. GODDARD wounded on duty. D. section relieved 4 guns of 141 Coy MGC in barrage positions at ZIEL HOUSE (Sheet 28 NE. T.7.a.4.b.) 8 O.R. attached as carrying party from each of 6th, 7th, 8th and 15th Battn. LONDON Regt.	
MONTREAL CAMP	27.8.17		Rain — Coy. moved to MONTREAL CAMP (Sheet 28 NW. H.19.b.6.7) — Casualties Nil.	
	28.8.17		Very windy; some rain	
	29.8.17		Dull	Dispositions unchanged. D section at ZIEL HOUSE. Transport at VANCOUVER CAMP. Remainder of Coy. at MONTREAL CAMP — Casualties Nil.
	30.8.17		Fair	
	31.8.17		Dull	

Rhynn Traylor CAPT
O.C. 140th COY. M.G. CORPS

Confidential.

Original War Diary

of

140th Company, Machine Gun Corps

for

September, 1917.

WAR DIARY

Army Form C. 2118.

Instructions regarding War Diaries and Intelligence Summaries are contained in F.S. Regs., Part II. and the Staff Manual respectively. Title pages will be prepared in manuscript.

INTELLIGENCE SUMMARY. 140th Machine Gun Company

(Erase heading not required.)

Place	Date 1917	Hour	Summary of Events and Information	Remarks and references to Appendices
	September 1.		Rain - Coy in billets at MONTREAL CAMP (M.19.d.6.7.- Sheet Belgium 28 N.W.). 32 men previously attached for carrying duty returned to their battalions. 3 O.R. joined from Base Depot. Transport lines shelled - 2 horses and 2 O.R. wounded.	Ref. Map Sheet Belgium 28 N.W.
	2.		2nd Section manning barrage guns at ZIEL HOUSE relieved by 4 guns of 195 M.G.Coy. - Casualties Nil.	
	3.		Guns - 47th Division transferred to Fifth Army. 6 guns relieved 6 guns of 25th Division for defence of dumps against enemy aircraft. 1 at H.14.b.5.8. ; 2 at G.29.d.9.4. ; 1 at H.13. central ; 2 at G.24.d.9.5. - Casualties Nil.	
	4.		Guns - 1 O.R. joined from Base Depot. 1 O.R. evacuated (sick) - Casualties Nil.	
	5.		Fine following storm during night. - 47th Division transferred from II Corps to I Anzac Corps. - Casualties Nil	
	6.		Duel stormy. - Capt. R.H. DRAYTON (O.C.Coy) to hospital and evacuated. - Casualties Nil.	
	7.		Fine - Casualties Nil.	
	8.		Guns - 6 guns employed on Anti-Aircraft work relieved by 6 Lewis guns of 1st Anzac Cyclist Batt. 140th Infantry Brigade relieved 7th Inf. Bde. in H.27.b.7.7. Company Hd D Section relieved 7th M.G.Coy at H.27.b.8.7.7. D.H. Stores and D Section remained at MONTREAL CAMP - Casualties Nil.	
	9.		Fine - 140th Infantry Brigade relieved 95th Inf. Bde. from CLAPHAM JUNCTION to J.8.C.4.6. Company less D Section relieved 95th M.G.Coy in line. Position of guns as follows:-	
			Anti front guns (A Section) 2 guns at J.14.a.80.50, left gun firing E. and b GLENCORSE WOOD, right gun firing S.S.E. along TARGON TRENCH and ml to FITZCLARENCE FARM.	
			Front line guns (A Section) 2 guns at J.14.a.26.30. having field of fire from S edge of GLENCORSE WOOD & INVERNESS COPSE	
			Barrage Guns (B & C Sections) 8 guns mounted at interval in JAMES TRENCH between J.13.a.50.80 and J.13.a.63.40. These guns were laid on fixed S.O.S. lines so as to form a barrage along a line drawn from J.8.d.80.10. to J.14.b.77.05. They were also used for harassing fire at nights on targets given by D.M.G.O. Casualties Nil.	

Army Form C. 2118.

WAR DIARY
INTELLIGENCE SUMMARY.
140th Machine Gun Company

(Erase heading not required.)

Place	Date 1917	Hour	Summary of Events and Information	Remarks and references to Appendices
Sept.	10		Line – Casualties Nil.	
	11.		Misty early, fine late. – 1 O.R. wounded at missing.	
	12.		Windy. – 2/Lt W. SMART joined from Base Depot. – Casualties Nil.	
	13.		Cloudy & windy. – O.M. Stres and D Section moved to VANCOUVER CAMP. D Section relieved A Section in out post and front line positions. – Casualties Nil.	
	14.		Fine. – Test S.O.S. took place along whole of 147th Bdl. front. Signals fired from H.Q. of 1/17th Batt. London Regt. Artillery fired. 1 round per battery on receipt of S.O.S. – Casualties Nil. Capt. C.E.W. DRUITT joined as O. Coy.	
	15.		Fine. – Gas projectors discharged in vicinity of WEST HOEK ridge between 2 a.m. & 5 a.m. Bombardment barrage by field guns and howitzers carried out between 9.30 a.m and 11.35 a.m and 4 p.m. to 4.42 p.m. During latter barrage the 17th Batt. London Regt. carried out a raid with 2 officers and 60 O.R. on German Strong Point about T. 14. C.7.8. Zero at 4 p.m. All objectives were gained and 36 prisoners taken, which number was increased on complete repulsion of German counter attack. Raiders' losses very slight. – 1 O.R. wounded.	
	16.		Barrages carried out as yesterday from 5.0 a.m. to 8.3 a.m. and 10.0 a.m. to 11.21 a.m. 140th Infantry Brigade relieved by units of 1st Australian Division. 8 barrage guns relieved by 8th Australian M.G. Coy., and 2 front line and 2 outpost guns relieved by 1st Australian M.G. Coy. Coy. returned to VANCOUVER CAMP. – 4 O.R. wounded. 1 O.R. evacuated (sick).	
	17.		Remainder of Brigade relieved by 1st Australian Division.	
	18.		Rainy. – Brigade moved to STEENVOORDE CENTRAL AREA. Company's billets and H.Q. at K. 2. b. a. 2. 1.	Ref. Map France Sheet 27
	19.		Fine – Casualties Nil. – Casualties Nil.	
	20.		Fine – Brigade moved to EEKE Area. Company's billets at farms at Q. 7. d. 9. 6. and Q. 7. b. 9. 1 (near STEENVOORDE) – Casualties Nil.	

Army Form C. 2118.

WAR DIARY or INTELLIGENCE SUMMARY.

140th Machine Gun Company.

(Erase heading not required.)

Place	Date 1917	Hour	Summary of Events and Information	Remarks and references to Appendices
Sept.	21		47th Division transferred from Second Army to First Army (XIII Corps) and moved by train. Company including Transport entrained at CAESTRE at 6.10 pm. - Casualties Nil	Ref. Map LENS 11 (1/100,000)
	22.		Company detrained at AUBIGNY (Pas de Calais) and marched to billets at AGNIERES. - Casualties Nil	
	23.		Company moved by march route to ANZIN - ST. AUBIN. - Casualties Nil	
	24.		Company moved by march route to (GAVRELLE). Coy. H.Q. at H.1.C.50.40. - Casualties Nil	
	25.		Company relieved 189 M.G. Coy in line.	
	26.		140th Infantry Brigade relieved 189th Inf. Bde. in line. — 1 O.R. wounded. Gun positions as follows:-	Ref. Map France Sheet 51B N.W.

Name of Map Position	Map Reference	
H.B.1.A.	H.6.b.15.50	
	H.6.b.20.60	
MB 1c	C.25.c.10.25	
MB 1d	C.25.c.14.31	
S1	B.30.c.50.65	
S2	B.30.c.45.75	
S3	B.30.a.50.15	
S4	B.30.a.55.55	
S5	B.24.d.10.38	
S6	B.24.d.12.70	
R1	H.5.a.85.60	
R2	H.5.a.55.65	
R3	B.28.d.62.82	
R4	B.29.a.05.50	
R5	B.29.a.08.65	
R6	B.29.a.10.80	

| | 26. | | Coy. Company H.Q. moved to H.5.a.50.65. During night firing carried on as follows:- MB 1 A gun on target C.27.C.04. (1500 rounds); MB 1 B gun on target C.27.C.20.65. (1500 rounds).- Casualties Nil. | |
| | 27. | | Dull early, fine later. - Destructive bombardment carried out by heavy artillery on trench from C.19.d.15.95 to C.19.d.28.65. M.G. fire carried out on night 27/28 by R3, R4, R5 & R6 guns on targets (i) CHEDDAR - C.19.b.15.75. (1250 rounds) (ii) LINK MAZE - C.13.d.20.30. (250 rounds) (iii) C.19.d.80.95 & C.20.a.10.10. (1000 rounds). - 1 O.R. rejoined Company. - Casualties Nil | |

Army Form C. 2118.

WAR DIARY
INTELLIGENCE SUMMARY.

140th Machine Gun Company.

(Erase heading not required.)

Instructions regarding War Diaries and Intelligence Summaries are contained in F.S. Regs., Part II. and the Staff Manual respectively. Title pages will be prepared in manuscript.

Place	Date 1917	Hour	Summary of Events and Information	Remarks and references to Appendices
Sept.	28		Fine. – M.G. fire carried out on night 28/29. (i) R.1 gun on target I.2.a.40.80. (1500 rounds). (ii) R.2 gun on C.26.c.50.45. (1000 rounds). (iii) R.3 gun on C.26.a.45.10. (1250 rounds) – Casualties Nil.	
	29		Cold, cloudy early. Destructive bombardment by heavies carried out on trench C.26.c.47.62 – C.26.c.67.00 at 3.15 p.m. On night 29/30, M.B.1 gun fired 3000 rounds on target (i) WAIT TRENCH (ii) GAVRELLE SUPPORT (iii) COUNT TRENCH (iv) CHUTNEY TRENCH (S. end). – Casualties Nil	
	30.		Fine. – F.1 gun moved to C.25.c.14.31. (New position called MB.1d.) Night 30/1st 3950 rounds fired. 600 rounds also fired on enemy aircraft. All elevating and traversing dials removed from tripods and handed over to 239th M.G. Coy.	

(Signature) R.H. Smith
CAPT.
O.C. 140th COY. M.G. CORPS

Confidential

Original War Diary
of
140th Machine Gun Company
for
October 1917.

140th Infantry Brigade

Herewith Original War Diary for the month of October, 1917.

[Stamp: 140 Machine Gun Company. Ref. No. MG/328. Date 1/11/17]

_____ CAPT.
O.C. 140th COY. M.G. CORPS.

WAR DIARY / INTELLIGENCE SUMMARY

Army Form C. 2118.

140th Machine Gun Company

Place	Date 1917	Hour	Summary of Events and Information	Remarks and references to Appendices
Field	Oct. 1		Ind.- Company still manning guns as shown on last month's diary in Right (GAVRELLE) Sub Sector of 47th Divisional front. During night 1/2 October, R1, R2 & R3 fired a total of 2700 rounds on targets in I.20.a, C.26.c, C.19.d, and C.25.b. 4 O.R. transferred to 239th M.G. Coy. 1 O.R. returned to Base Depot (inefficient). 3 men previously attached from Infantry for preliminary duty returned to their Battalion. — Casualties Nil.	Ref. France Sheet 51b N.W.
	2.		Ind.- During night 2/3rd Oct. 1 gun of R Section fired 3000 rounds from C.25.C.85.15 on targets in C.28.b, I.3.b., C.27.d and C.27.b. — Casualties Nil.	
	3.		Ind.- 140th Infantry Brigade relieved by 141st Infantry Brigade. Company returned by lorry to the billets at MILLHOUSE, ANZIN ST AUBIN. — Casualties Nil.	
	4.		Dull, heavy storm in evening.— During the period the following training was carried out:- Physical Training; Gun Drill in Six Respirators and P.H. Helmets; Company Drill; Barrage Drill; Immediate Actions; Sports. All belts, ammunition, guns and gun equipment were thoroughly cleaned and overhauled. Coy. was also bathed and paid. — Casualties Nil.	
	5.		Dull. Some rain.— 4 O.R. Brit. Artillery relieved 63rd Brit. Arty on nights 4/5th Oct.— 1 O.R. evacuated.	
	6.		Rain.	
	7.		Dull, Rain.	
	8.		Fine early, heavy rain later.— Draft 1 O.R. joined	
	9.		Fair early, rain in evening.—	
	10.		Dull, cold, rain in morning.— 140th Infantry Brigade in Left (OPPY) Sub Sector of 47th Divl. Divnl. Company entrained at MILLHOUSE, ANZIN, at 4.45am, detrained at ASHFORD JUNCTION, and relieved guns of 142nd M.G. Coy as shown in Appendix I. — Casualties Nil.	
	11.		Ind. Coy.- At 3am. gun was discharged from firedown in vicinity of MARQUIS TRENCH (B.18.a.9.1) against enemy's position in C.13.b, and C.7.d. (OPPY SUPPORT, OPPY VILLAGE and CRUCIFIX TRENCH). Reliable reports state that German 50th Infantry Regt. suffered considerable casualties. 350 rounds fired at hostile aircraft from R7 and R9 positions — Casualties Nil.	

Army Form C. 2118.

WAR DIARY
INTELLIGENCE SUMMARY.   140th Machine Gun Company.
(Erase heading not required.)

Instructions regarding War Diaries and Intelligence Summaries are contained in F. S. Regs., Part II. and the Staff Manual respectively. Title pages will be prepared in manuscript.

Place	Date 1917	Hour	Summary of Events and Information	Remarks and references to Appendices
Oct	12		War Range. — Night 11/12th, MB 2a & 2b guns fired 500 rounds on LINK MAZE and tracks in C.19.b. — Casualties Nil.	
	13		Bright generally, rain in evening. — Night 12/13th, MB 2a & 2b guns fired 1000 rounds on C.14.a. 25.40. Between 8pm and 10 pm gas was projected by Capt (310?) Division against further portion of ACHEVILLE. Artillery fired 400 rounds of 6" against OPPY SUPPORT and Coy (?) co-operated, LINK MAZE and CHALK PIT being searched. 93rd Inf. Bde. relieved 92nd Inf. Bde. in Right Sub-Sector of 31st Div. front. 1/17th London Regt. relieved 1/19th London Regt. in Right Sub-Sector of 147th Bde. front. — Casualties Nil. Gun C.21. — the rifle robbing expired between midnight and 1 a.m. to deal with which S14, S8, MB 2a and MB 2b guns fired 1450 rounds of enemy aircraft. 182nd Inf. Bde. (R.I. Div.) raided enemy trenches R9 & R9 guns fired 380 rounds of enemy aircraft. 182nd Inf. Bde. (R.I. Div.) raided enemy trenches in I.14.c. with Artillery & Trench Mortar co-operation. German message tapped stating that they propose to retaliate for our gas projection on OPPY by a Trench Mortar Gas bombardment. — Casualties Nil.	
	14.		Frosty, Bright. — Night 14/15th MB 2a & 2b, MB 2a & 2b and S14 guns fired 2250 rounds on C.13.b., C.20.a., and C.8.c. — Casualties Nil.	
	15.		Bright. Little rain in evening. — Night 15/16th, MB 2a, 2b and S13 guns fired 1950 rounds on C.15.d., C.20.b. and C.14.b. Heavy Arty. fired 300 rounds of 6" on CHESTNUT TRENCH from C.19.d. 55.60. 16R Coy co-operated firing also on CRUET. 18R Regt Coy. b take C.19.d. 50.10. 141st M.G. Coy (on right) co-operated firing also on CRUET. 18R Regt for Advanced M.G. Course at GRANTHAM. — Casualties Nil. at Commission. 10R Regt for Advanced M.G. Course at GRANTHAM. — Casualties Nil.	
	16		Bright. — S13 gun fired 2000 rounds on C.14.b.0.9. and C.8.b.9.9 during night 16/17th. — Casualties Nil.	
	17		June. — 3.30 am 141st Bde. raided enemy's trenches between C.19.d.15.40 and C.19.d.10.75. H.G. Co-operation programme, see Appendix 2. R9, MB 2a & 2.b. S4, S8, S14 guns fired 14,250 rounds on C.20.a., C.19.B., & 20.a., C.25.B., C.19.d. and C.13.R. Raiders found enemy trenches very lightly held. 9 Germans were killed and 1 prisoner brought back. Raiders casualties slight.	
	18			

Army Form C. 2118.

WAR DIARY
or
INTELLIGENCE SUMMARY.

(Erase heading not required.)

140th Machine Gun Company

Instructions regarding War Diaries and Intelligence Summaries are contained in F. S. Regs., Part II. and the Staff Manual respectively. Title pages will be prepared in manuscript.

Place	Date 1917	Hour	Summary of Events and Information	Remarks and references to Appendices
Oct.	18 (Cont'd).		141st Inf. Bde. relieved by 142nd Inf. Bde. in Right Sub-Sector of Oct. front. 1/15th London Regt. relieved 1/14th London Regt. in Right of Brigade front and 1/6th London Regt. relieved 1/8th London Regt. in Left of Brigade front. 1/19th Batt. proceeded to SUPPORT and 1/8th to RESERVE. R7 & R9 guns fired 860 rounds against enemy aircraft. — Casualties Nil.	
	19.		Bull. — S15 gun fired 250 rounds at enemy aircraft. 1 O.R. transferred to 141st M.G. Coy. 2 O.R. evacuated (Sick). — Casualties Nil.	
	20.		Cloudy, bright and cold. — Night 19/20th, S14, S9, S10, S7 and S8 fired 7500 rounds on C.20.b., C.14.c. and C.20.d. R9 gun fired 2000 rounds at enemy aircraft. — Casualties Nil.	
	21.		Cloudy, Dull. — Night 20/21st, F2, S7 and S8 guns fired 6000 rounds on C.8.c., C.15.a., and C.15.c. and R9 and S5 guns fired 290 rounds at enemy aircraft. S13 gun 2250 rounds on C.7.b and C.13.b. — Casualties Nil. 1 O.R. to U.K. for Commission. — Casualties Nil.	
	22.		Fair. — Night 21/22nd, S7 and S10 guns fired 2000 rounds on C.20.b. and C.14.c. at 6.15 pm Right Brigade of 31st (?) Division carried out gas projectors against FRESNOY PARK and VILLAGE, accompanied by desultory artillery fire to deaden sound of projectors. — 1 O.R. evacuated (sick). — Casualties Nil.	
	23.		Dull morning, fair later. — Night 22/23rd, S7, S8 and S13 guns fired 5500 rounds on C.13.b, C.20.b., C.7.b and C.7.d. — Casualties Nil.	
	24.		Fine, cool, some rain in evening. Night firing (23/24th); S7, S10 and R9 guns fired 5120 rounds on C.1.d., C.7.c., C.7.a., C.13.b. — Casualties Nil. Eve. — Night 24/25th. 184th Inf. Bde. (61st Div.) raided enemy trenches on I.1.d. and I.2.c. 141, 500 rounds fired on C.7.a, C and C.20.a., C.19.b., C.13.a. yd. by 10 of Coys guns. 93rd Inf. Bde. relieved 93rd Infantry Brigade in Rt. Sub. Sector of 31st Div. Front at 4 pm. gas cases projected from vicinity of BOYNE STREET against enemy positions on C.7.a & C. (FRESNOY TRENCH and CRUCIFIX LANE) 3 Bearers joined from Adv. Horsed Transport Depot. — Casualties Nil	

Army Form C. 2118.

WAR DIARY
or
INTELLIGENCE-SUMMARY.
(Erase heading not required.)

140th Machine Gun Company

Instructions regarding War Diaries and Intelligence Summaries are contained in F.S. Regs., Part II. and the Staff Manual respectively. Title pages will be prepared in manuscript.

Place	Date 1917	Hour	Summary of Events and Information	Remarks and references to Appendices
Oct	26.		Wed.- Night 25/26th. P of Coys guns fired 12,500 rounds on C.13.a.b.d. C.14.a., and C.7.a. and 140th Infantry Brigade relieved by 141st Inf. Bde. Company relieved by 141 M.G. Coy and returned to Mill House ANKIN ST AUBIN by lorry. – Casualties Nil	
	27. 28. 29. 30. 31.		Thur.} Fri.} Gun & Grocery} drill early, Rival later.} Gun early, train later.} Fine} During this period the Coy. was billeted and paid; gun equipment thoroughly overhauled & cleaned; barrage drill, range work (stoppages) and physical training carried out; all box respirators which had not been tested in a gas chamber were so tested. 1 Section also carried out work on transport lines. — Casualties Nil	

[Signature]
CAPT.
O.C. 140th COY. M.G. CORPS.

Appendix 1.

Guns manned by 140th M.G. Coy. in OPPY
Sector during period 10th - 26th October, 1917.

F3 at B.24.d.80.90. RAILWAY TRENCH
F2 at B.24.b.45.45. BLUE ALLEY

Both of these fire towards the WINDMILL and are intended to defend the line MARINE TRENCH — EARL TRENCH — MARQUIS TRENCH.

S7 at B.24.b.25.20. } MARINE TRENCH. These cross fire behind the 2 F. guns.
S8 at B.24.b.30.25.
S9 at B.18.d.10.17.   EARL TRENCH.   Fires across F2.
S10 at B.18.d.15.20. EARL TRENCH.   Fires on to OPPY WOOD.
S11 at B.18.c.80.90. SOUTH DUKE STREET. Fires on N. corner of OPPY WOOD.
S12 at B.18.a.60.00. DUKE STREET. Cross-fires with S10 behind S11.
S13 at B.12.c.40.05. MARQUIS TRENCH. Fires N.E.
S14 at B.12.c.05.10. KENT ROAD.   Cross-fires with S11
S15 at B.18.c.30.05. OUSE ALLEY. Cross-fires with S12

All these guns defend line MARINE TRENCH — EARL TRENCH — MARQUIS TRENCH.

Red Line

R7 B.23.c.90.80. BAILLEUL EAST.   Fires S.E.   } The object of these
R8 B.23.a.80.30.   do   do   } Crossing Fire } guns is to defend
R9 B.17.c.65.35. off OUSE ALLEY   } the RED LINE.

Mobile Battery

MB 2a }
MB 2b } B.24.a.70.10.

These intended for sniping in co-operation with artillery

Note. S15, R7 and R9 guns are mounted against aircraft by day.

Appendix 2

SECRET.

Programme for the Co-operation of Machine Guns in the
Raid by 17th Battn., Lon Regt., on the night 17th/18th October.

Gun Position.		Area fired on.	Time.
M.B.1a. M.B.1b.	H.6.b.15.50.	(a). CRUET TRENCH, C.19.d.85.85. to C.20.a.30.40. (b). CHESTNUT TRENCH and junctions with CRUET and CHOP.	Zero to zero plus 20 minutes. Zero plus 20 to zero plus 31.
M.B.1d.	C.25.c.20.30.	CRUET TRENCH, C.19.d.85.85. to C.20.a.30.40.	Zero to zero plus 31.
R.1 R.2	From night firing positions.	CHUTNEY and CRAB, C.19.d.50.20. to C.25.b.65.30.	Zero to zero plus 31.
M.B.2a. M.B.2b.	B.24.a.70.10.		
S.9 S.10 S.11 S.12.	B.18.d.20.20. B.18.c.80.80. B.18.a.55.10.	CHEDDAR TRENCH C.19.b.20.70. to C.19.b.50.00.	Zero to zero plus 31.
S.3 S.4.	B.30.a.60.65. B.30.a.40.40.	GAVRELLE SUPPORT.	Zero to zero plus 31.
S.7 S.8	B.24.b.80.20. B.24.b.25.35.	Junction of CRUMB & CHALK TRENCHES.	Zero to zero plus 31.

RATE OF FIRE :-

Guns to fire at barrage rate (1 belt per four minutes).

Confidential.

Original War Diary
of
140th Machine Gun Company
for
November 1917.

140 Infantry Brigade

Herewith Original War Diary of the
Coy. for November 1917.

140 Machine
Gun Company.
Ref. No. MG/434
Date 6.12.17

C.E.H. [signature]
                    CAPT
O.C. 140th Coy. M.G. [...]

Army Form C. 2118.

WAR DIARY / INTELLIGENCE SUMMARY

140th Machine Gun Company

November 1917

(Erase heading not required.)

Instructions regarding War Diaries and Intelligence Summaries are contained in F. S. Regs., Part II. and the Staff Manual respectively. Title pages will be prepared in manuscript.

Place	Date	Hour	Summary of Events and Information	Remarks and references to Appendices
ANZIN-ST-AUBIN near ARRAS	1.11.17 2.11.17 3.11.17 4.11.17		Coy in Reserve at MILL HOUSE, ANZIN. Casualties Nil.	Maps Sheet 51B 1/40,000
MB at H5a.55.55 Sheet 51B	5.11.17		142 Inf.Bde. raided enemy trenches in C25.b. and d. in afternoon, 12 guns of this Coy. co-operated, firing 1 belt per gun per 4 minutes from Zero to Zero + 60. From Zero + 60 to Zero + 90, bursts of 100 rounds per gun every 5 mins. Casualties Nil	
	6.11.17 7.11.17 8.11.17		140 Inf.Bde. relieved 142 Inf.Bde. 140 M.G.Coy relieved 142 M.G.Coy in right section of the Divisional Front. Casualties Nil. 2 Officers & 24 other ranks & establishment of M.G. Bart. Sep.to C 26 a 00.80. Casualties Nil. Keeping the night 5/6 one gun fired 750 rounds from B 29 d 25.45 on to C26 a 30.70. Casualties Nil During the night 6/7 six guns fired 14000 rounds on enemy's tracks and trenches. Casualties Nil During night 7/8, 2500 rounds fired on C 25 b. 20.80, C 19 b. 80.50 and C 26 a 30.70. At 12 noon, 3/st Divr.(on our left) raided enemy trenches in T24b and d at U19c. 2 guns of one section from positions R1 and R2 mounted to THAMES BATTERY positions and 2 guns of another section from positions S3 and S4 mounted to THAMES BATTERY. Rate of fire = 100 per gun per minute from Zero to Zero + 30 and 75 per minute from Zero + 30 to Zero + 45. 3500 rounds were fired at C13 d 6.9. 2500 rounds on C13 d 81. 2500 rounds on C 20 a.99 and 1000 on C13 d 9.6. Enemy artillery retaliated on the Battery. Casualties Nil	
	9.11.17		4th Canadian relieved 15th London in Right Front. 8th London relieved 6th London in Left Front. Coy moved to support. 15th Bn. moved to Reserve. Casualties Nil.	
	10.11.17 11.11.17		4500 rounds fired on enemy trenches during night of 9/10th. Casualties Nil. During night 10/11, one gun fired 750 rounds on C26 d 6.9, another gun fired 450 rounds on C 27 d 3.0. Casualties Nil	
	12.11.17 13.11.17		Night firing on night 11/12 ch = 2500 rounds fired by 3 guns on enemy's tracks & trenches. 142 Inf. Bde. took over old Divisional front under ??? Post Scheme. 140 Inf. Bde moved back into support. 142 M.G. Coy relieved certain guns of this Coy; the remainder were withdrawn into Brigade action named TYNE BATTERY and one to THAMES BATTERY 21B and one to RAILWAY CUTTING, B 27 a.0.14. Casualties Nil	relieved or withdrawn and ...

Army Form C. 2118.

WAR DIARY

INTELLIGENCE SUMMARY.

(Erase heading not required.)

140th Machine Gun Company

November 1917.

Instructions regarding War Diaries and Intelligence Summaries are contained in F.S. Regs., Part II and the Staff Manual respectively. Title pages will be prepared in manuscript.

Place	Date	Hour	Summary of Events and Information	Remarks and references to Appendices
RAILWAY CUTTING	14.11.17		2 Lieuts at RAILWAY CUTTING changed guns, clothing and equipment. Baths during morning. Casualties Nil.	
B.27.a.0.4. Shut 51B	15.11.17		Dispositions unchanged. Casualties Nil.	
	16.11.17		16 O.R. (being gunners) attached from Infantry of the Brigade to replace men away from unit. Casualties Nil. Sections at H.Q. relieved sections at THAMES and TYNE BATTERIES reported. 1 O.R. evacuated.	
	17.11.17		1 O.R. (A.S.M.) joined from 27 Coy. M.G.C. Casualties Nil.	
MONT ST ELOY	18.11.17		Brigade relieved by 92 Inf. Bde. and moved into Corps Reserve about ECOIVRES. Coy. relieved by 92 M.G. Coy. with the exception of 4 guns left in RAILWAY CUTTING. Coy. moved together with transport to MONT ST ELOY, personnel by train from GUN JUNCTION to ECOIVRES and transport by road. 1 O.R. joined from Base Depot. 1 Spl. proceeded to Base Depot for a course at GRANTHAM (M.G.T.C.) Casualties Nil.	
	19.11.17		Remaining 4 guns relieved at RAILWAY CUTTING and rejoined Coy. Casualties Nil.	
	20.11.17		Guns, clothing and equipment cleaned. Baths at ECOIVRES. Casualties Nil.	
GOUVES	21.11.17		Brigade moved by march route to HERMAVILLE area. Coy. moved to GOUVES. Billeted in huts and tents. Casualties Nil. 1 O.R. evacuated.	
SIMENCOURT	22.11.17		Brigade moved by march route to WANQUETIN - SIMENCOURT area. Coy. moved to huts in Short LU. SIMENCOURT. Casualties Nil.	
	23.11.17		Company resting at SIMENCOURT.	
COURCELLES - LE COMTE	24.11.17		Brigade moved to COURCELLES - LE COMTE area by march route. Coy. in huts and bivouacs at COURCELLES - LE COMTE. 3 O.R. rejoined from hospital. Casualties Nil.	
BEAULENCOURT	25.11.17		Brigade moved by march route to BEAULENCOURT area. Coy. moved to huts in BEAULENCOURT. 1 O.R. Camp. Casualties Nil.	
	26.11.17		Coy. resting at BEAULENCOURT. 32 O.R. joined from Infantry as Carriers. Casualties Nil.	
DOIGNIES	27.11.17		Brigade moved by lorries to LEBUCQUIERE, thence by march route to DOIGNIES. Transport moved by road. Casualties Nil.	

Army Form C. 2118.

140th Machine Gun Coy.
November 1917

WAR DIARY
INTELLIGENCE SUMMARY.
(Erase heading not required.)

Place	Date	Hour	Summary of Events and Information	Remarks and references to Appendices
DOIGNIES	28.11.17		Coy. moved from DOIGNIES and C Section relieved 8 guns of 212th M.G. Coy. Sut of BOURLON WOOD. B and D Sections remained in reserve at Rear Coy. H.Q. at K.6.a.6.9 (Thug 57.c) Casualties Nil.	Disposition of guns shown attached
BOURLON WOOD near CAMBRAI	29.11.17		BOURLON WOOD, GRAINCOURT and SUGAR FACTORY at E.29.a.6.8.7.3 heavily bombarded with gas & H.E. shells.	
	30.11.17		Enemy began early with machine gun shell bombardment of BOURLON WOOD, GRAINCOURT, SUGAR FACTORY and whole of his system on whole side of the wood. SUGAR FACTORY received special attention. Later the bombardment changed to H.E. During the morning the enemy made several attacks but were repulsed. About 2.30 to 3 p.m. he again attacked. The 2nd Americans on our left were driven back, freeing the North London Regt. to give ground. 2 guns of A Section were run off or destroyed, the teams being missing. Privates ? guns destroyed by shell fire. The and gun of A Section was started to be 25 sd, the may, to come. A Counter attack reclaimed part of the lost ground, leaving enemy front line about 150-200 yards in advance of his original line. During the day C Section repeatedly engaged the enemy and kept fire at a range of about 600 yards causing very heavy casualties. B and D Sections proceeded to the line arriving at Adv. Coy. H.Q. in the SUGAR FACTORY at 8 p.m. Casualties: 1 Offr. and 2 O.R. killed, 4 O.R. wounded, 11 O.R. missing.	

C.S.H. Smith
Capt.
O.C. 140 M.G. Coy.

Ref MOEUVRES 1/20,000   H.C.5

M.G. Dispositions 8am 29.11.17

A Sect.   HQ at E.15.c.6.2
     1 Gun at E.18.c.6.1 firing N.W.
     1 Gun at E.18.c.6.3   "   N.E.
     1 Gun at E.12.c.6.0 approx firing from N & WNW
     1 Gun in reserve at Section HQ

I propose to take this gun tonight to on the gun at E.12.c.6.0 about 150x to the left so as to provide cross fire covering the approaches to the village and the valley in E.11.

C Section   HQ at E.17.d.4.1
     1 gun at E.17.d.30.3½ firing N
     1 gun at E.17.d.30.15 firing NW
     1 gun at E.23.b.7.8 firing W.N.W.
     1 gun at E.23.b.75.85 firing E.

Advanced Coy HQ Sugar Factory E.29.a.68.73
Rear Coy HQ ~~K.16.a.6.7~~ and 2 Sections (reserve) at K.16.a.6.7

All guns have either 2000 or 2500 rounds in belts with a reserve of respectively 2000 & 1000. This reserve will be raised tonight to 3000 per gun

            Lt. C.E.H Druitt Capt
29.11.17   Cmdg 116 Coy, M.G.C.

Confidential

Original War Diary
of
140th Machine Gun Company
for
December 1917.

Army Form C. 2118.

140th Machine Gun Company
December 1917

WAR DIARY
or
INTELLIGENCE SUMMARY.
(Erase heading not required.)

Instructions regarding War Diaries and Intelligence Summaries are contained in F. S. Regs., Part II. and the Staff Manual respectively. Title pages will be prepared in manuscript.

Place	Date	Hour	Summary of Events and Information	Remarks and references to Appendices
BOURLON WOOD near CAMBRAI	1.12.17		Sugar Factory at E.29.a & 68.73 Guns bombarded at 2.30 p.m. Wegns received from Divisional Commander thanking all ranks for the bravery & the gallant and steady manner in which they repulsed the enemy's attacks. Nil casualties.	
	2.12.17		About 4.15 p.m. violent artillery activity on left of Bn. front, spreading later to BOURLON WOOD. At 8.10 p.m. a counter attack by 17th and 186th Batns London Regt. supported by M.G. barrage fire by D Section regained most of the ground lost on 30th ult. The enemy being driven off the ridge except at one point. 11 M.Gs. were put through. 1 gun of B Section was disposed of by shell fire. Casualties – 1 O.R. killed & 1 O.R. wounded.	
	3.12.17		Dispositions unchanged. No events of importance. 1 O.R. wounded (gas)	Report Rejoined on 3.12.17
	4.12.17		On night 4/5th to shorten line, the 47th Division and the Division on each flank withdrew by stages to main line. The withdrawal was covered by 1/15th Batt London Regt. supported by the 4 guns of B Section. Casualties – 1 O.R. accidentally injured and 1 O.R. wounded.	
			Dispositions unchanged. 3 O.R. wounded (gas). 2 O.R. (gas) joined	
	5.12.17		1 O.R. wounded (gas)	
	6.12.17		4 O.R. joined. 1 O.R. accidentally injured.	
	7.12.17		1 O.R. wounded (gas)	
	8.12.17			
	9.12.17		From K.23.b. Harassing fire was brought to bear on K.4.d area from 7 p.m. to 4 a.m. 10,750 rounds being fired in all. 2 O.R. (gas) to Base Depot for transfer to England. 4 O.R. joined. 1 O.R. evacuated sick.	
	10.12.17		1/20th Ldn London Regt. relieved 1/6th and 1/7th Bns London Regts. At 4 a.m. C Section firing from K.22.b. brought down an enemy aeroplane at K.3 central. 1 Officer joined. 4 Lewis Gunners of each of 1/7th, 1/8th and 1/15th London Regts. returned to their Batns.	
	11.12.17		Brigade Com. M.G. Coy. relieved by 141 Bde. Harassing fire from K.22.b was brought to bear on K.4.d from 8.0 p.m. to 12 midnight. 15 H.a.m. and at K.4.d from K.5.a and K.6.c from 6.30 p.m. to 12 midnight. 1 O.R. wounded. 1 sick.	
	12.12.17		Coy. relieved by 141 M.G. Coy and moved to BERTINCOURT. H.Q. at P.7.6.3. (Sheet 57c). 2 O.R's evac. sick.	

Army Form C. 2118.

140 Machine Gun Company
December 1917.

WAR DIARY
or
INTELLIGENCE SUMMARY.
(Erase heading not required)

Instructions regarding War Diaries and Intelligence Summaries are contained in F. S. Regs., Part II. and the Staff Manual respectively. Title pages will be prepared in manuscript.

Place	Date	Hour	Summary of Events and Information	Remarks and references to Appendices
BERTINCOURT	13.12.17		Coy resting at BERTINCOURT. 1 Runner & 1/6th London, 5 carriers & 1/17th London, 1 cooker & 1/18th London and 7 carriers of 1/19th London rejoined their Batns. 2 ORs wounded & sick.	
	14.12.17		Refitting carried out. Roman Catholic Service at 9.0 am.	
	15.12.17		Refitting continued. 2 guns on anti-aircraft work at YTRES Railhead relieved by 2 guns of 54 Division Bgde.	
Coy HQ at K15 d.2.2 Hut 57c	16.12.17		Coy proceeded to the line and relieved 2 guns of the 141 M.G. Coy in K16 d.4.6. 2 guns of 141 Coy at K11 c.0.8 and K10 d.1.1. 4 guns of 258 Coy (not 141 Coy) at K10 c.7.1. and 4 guns of 142 Coy (No 2 Battery) at K15 b1.9. Coy HQ taken over from 258 M.G. Coy at K15 d.2.2. Casualties Nil.	
	17.12.17		Harassing fire carried on - 108 rounds fired.	
	18.12.17		Harassing fire during day - 1500 rounds on K5 d.4.2. 1000 rounds on K5 c.1.7. Harassing fire on night 18/19 - 1000 rounds on K4 d.6.5. 1000 rounds on K4 b.5.5. Casualties Nil.	
	19.12.17		Day firing - 2000 rounds on K5 d.4.2 and 1125 rounds on K5 c.1.7. Night harassing fire on 19/20 as follows:- 1250 rounds on K4 d.1.4. 1000 rounds on K5 d.4.3. 2750 rounds on K4 b.5.5. 1800 rounds on K22 c.2.2. and 1550 rounds on K3 a.9.5. Casualties Nil.	
	20.12.17		Harassing fire on night 20/21 - 1000 rounds on K6 b.5.5 and 4000 rounds on K5 c.1.7. Casualties Nil.	
BERTINCOURT	21.12.17		Coy relieved by 516 Coy M.G.C. and moved to BERTINCOURT.	
	22.12.17		Coy proceeded by light railway to ETRICOURT, MERICOURT and marched to billets at HEILLY.	
HEILLY	23.12.17		Coy cleaned clothing & equipment. Refitting commenced.	
	24.12.17		Refitting continued. Refitting commenced. Rifles inspected by Section Officers.	
	25.12.17		Guns & equipment cleaned. Refitting continued.	
	26.12.17		Church parade at RIBEMONT.	
	27.12.17		Coy carried out instruction in machine gun stoppages and Lewis Gun. Box Respirator Drill. 60 inspected at 10.30 am.	
	28.12.17		Section Officers instructed their Sections in the American Lock march from 10.30 am to 1 pm. 1 Officer joined from leave Sept 7.	
	29.12.17		Instruction in Fire Direction & Physical Training. 20 notified boys at 12.30 pm.	
	30.12.17		Box Respirator & Rifle inspection. Anti-Gas training relieved 8.45 - 13 joined.	
	31.12.17		Coy moved by Motor Lorries from HEILLY to RIBEMONT. 1 OR (1599) to One Bn for Duty for leave in England.	

Reading, Physical Training, Revolver Exercises instruction in Gas Drill in first Divisional Reserves.

A/OC 140th Coy M.G. CORPS

To 140th Inf. Bde.

    M.G. Dispositions   3.12.17

1 Section in Sunken Road about E.17.d.4.1

1 Section in Trench E.30.a.4.7

1 Section in Gun Pits E.29.d.7.6 (3 guns)

As 255 Coy have now made their Section at E.23.d.10 up to strength (4 guns), I shall withdraw the gun I had attached to them and shall send it to complete the Section in E.29.d tonight.

    The spare personnel I shall send back to rear H.Q, where, as soon as they have drawn another gun, there will be 1 complete section in reserve.

2.50 pm   (Sd) C.H. Dewitt Capt
3.12.17   OC 140th Coy., M.G.C

Casualties Killed

				Tde	Base
2/Lt	Stewart (30/11/17)			1/12/17	1/12/17
	Lemon (6th)	30/11/17		1/12/17	1/12/17
	Cossar (A)	30/11/17		1/12/17	1/12/17
2/C	Crowley (B)	2/12/17		3/12/17	3/12/17

Vol 25

Confidential

Original War Diary
of
140th Machine Gun Company
for
January 1918

140 Machine
Gun Company.
Ref. No
Date

WAR DIARY or INTELLIGENCE SUMMARY

Army Form C. 2118.

140 Machine Gun Company

January 1918

Place	Date	Hour	Summary of Events and Information	Remarks and references to Appendices
HEILLY nr. ALBERT (SOMME)	1.1.18		Company carried out gun cleaning, Combined Drill, Judging Distance, Visual Training and Range Cards and Physical Training.	
	2.1.18		A + B Sections carried out Range Firing, 2nd & 3rd Line instruction on the Direction (use of compass), followed by Physical Training, Combined Drill, and Preparing Stoppages in belts for range. Elementary Squad paraded with 20 Infantry.	
	3.1.18		Company carried out gun cleaning at the Route march (Fighting order). I.O.R. joined Company. Practiced for gun cleaning Belt filling & cleaning, Picketing guns, limbering up, overhauling gun equipment, Physical Training, The Direction when taken officers.	
	4.1.18		and Elementary Squad no work. I.O.R. joined.	
	5.1.18		C + D Sections paraded for work in training area (D 21 c.m.) to practice coming into action involving use of (12) mule animals. A + B Sections carried out the Direction (use of compass), Physical Training, Combined Drill and Judging Distance (visual training), Range Cards, working at V1 a.5.2.	
	6.1.18		Company attended Divine Service, dress puttees with belts worn outside. I.O.R. evacuated.	
	7.1.18		A + B Sections paraded to look over Pack Saddles, cleaned guns and carried out training on D21c1d. C + D Sections cleaned guns, were instructed on Theory of Barrage Drill, Physical Training, Barrage Drill and Prepared belts for stoppages when Range Firing. A + B Sections overhauled Pack saddles, cleaned guns and carried out work in training area D21c1d. C + D Sections carried out Range Firing. I.O.R. wounded.	
	8.1.18		C + D Sections carried out Gun cleaning, Barrage Drill, Physical Training, Immediate Action in Gas Helmets, Rifle Bolt instruction and had a lecture on "Discipline and Esprit de Corps". A + B Sections overhauled Pack saddles, cleaned guns and carried out work on training area D21c1d – practiced coming into action involving use of pack animals. Elementary squad carried out elementary practice and stoppages on the range in D16d.	
	9.1.18			

WAR DIARY
INTELLIGENCE SUMMARY

Army Form C. 2118.

140 Machine Gun Company
January 1918.

Place	Date	Hour	Summary of Events and Information	Remarks and references to Appendices
HEILLY.	10.1.18.		Company cleared billets, parked limbers and marched to MERICOURT L'ABBE Station; entrained, and detrained at ETRICOURT; then proceeded by route march to billets in BERTINCOURT.	
BERTINCOURT.	11.1.18.		Company paraded for overhauling belts and cleaning guns.	
	12.1.18.		Company paraded under Section Officers and were at their disposal.	
	13.1.18.		Company paraded to park limbers and were afterwards the Officers and N.C.O's were given a lecture by Lt. Goddard. Company relieved the 142 M.G. Coy in the line in the evening. Casualties nil. Coy. H.Q. 2 the catacombs RIBECOURT. Disposition of Sections in Battery. "A" Battery - "C" Section. "B" Battery - "C" Section.	Ref. map. NEWWOOD 1/10,000. L25a,75.05. "A" Battery. L26 & 10.15 "B" Battery L20c.35.20 "C" Battery. L19d.12.72 Reserve Section. K36b.15.42
RIBECOURT	14.1.18.		"D" Sec. "B" Section was in reserve and guns mounted for anti-aircraft firing. Situation normal. Little artillery activity. Casualties nil. Relief DAGO TRENCH PREMY SWITCH.	
	15.1.18		RIBECOURT lightly shelled, clearing up of trenches done by sections. Casualties nil.	
	16.1.18		RIBECOURT frequently bombarded chiefly to the BRASSERIE and batteries. Trenches revetted in places by sections. Casualties nil.	
	17.1.18		Work done on a-aircraft positions by "B" Section. Company supplied small working parties to assist tunnellers. "A" Section relieved "C" Section at dusk. "A" & "B" Batteries linked up to Right Battn. & to Coy. H.Q. by telephone. A,B,& C Batteries linked up; also "C" Battery to Centre Battn. Two guns of "C" Battery carried out Harassing Fire from 6p.m. to 1 a.m. — 500 rounds on L164d.9.4. 2500 rounds on roads & tracks in L.15a. Casualties nil.	
	18.1.18.		Two guns of "A" Batt. carried out Harassing Fire from 6 p.m. to 1 a.m on roads in L.22a. leading up to PREMY CHAPEL. Enemy Aircraft engaged by Reserve Section, 250 rounds fired. 3500 rounds fired during night. Casualties nil.	
	19.1.18.		Enemy artillery very active 6-9 p.m. "B" Sec. relieved "D" Sec. at dusk. 9 O.Rs joined. Casualties Nil.	

WAR DIARY
INTELLIGENCE SUMMARY

Army Form C. 2118.

140 Machine Gun Company

January 1918.

Place	Date	Hour	Summary of Events and Information	Remarks and references to Appendices
NINEWOOD	20.1.18		Neighbourhood of RIBECOURT CHURCH heavily shelled 10.30–12.30 p.m. Work continued in cleaning trenches etc. by autons. Casualties 1 O.R. wounded.	
	21.1.18		"C" Battery supplied carrying party for tunnellers. Two guns of "A" Battery carried out harassing fire from 6 p.m. to 1 a.m. on L.15 d 2, L.16 c 1.3 r 4, L.22 r 1 r 4. – 3500 rounds fired. Casualties nil.	
	22.1.18		"C" section relieved "A" Section at dusk. Two guns of "C" Battery carried out harassing fire from 6 p.m. to 1 a.m. on L.15 a 1 r 2, L.5 d 2 r 3, L.8 a 2 r 3, 3500 rounds were fired. "C" Battery supplied a carrying party for tunnellers. & deepened and drained trench. Casualties 1 O.R. wounded (gas)	
	23.1.18		Two guns of "A" Battery fired 3,000 rounds on L.16 c 1.3 r 4, ¾ L.15 d. 2 from 6.30 p.m. to 1 a.m. Harassing fire. Work continued on digging & supplies for tunnellers by autons in accord. Casualties 1 O.R. wounded at duty.	
	24.1.18		1000 rounds fired as harassing fire following up an R.E.8. Working party supplies for tunnellers by autons in accord. Casualties nil.	
	25.1.18		Company relieved at dusk by the 141.00 M.G. Coy. and proceeded to TRESCAULT where they entrained on the light railway to BERTINCOURT and took over billets.	
BERTINCOURT	26.1.18		Company paraded for cleaning guns and kits; anti-aircraft defence positions taken by the 141 & G Coy. Casualties nil.	
	27.1.18		Company handed to Divine Service. Military Cross ribbon presented to Capt. E.A. Druitt (Coy) Lieut. H. Paramo (2nd i/c) and military medal ribbon to 44522 Sgt. J. Dunn 975185 Pte. H Connah by General Jennings.	
	28.1.18		Company paraded for general cleaning equipment cleaning and the M.O. to form a lecture.	
	29.1.18		Company paraded for erecting splinter proof shelter round their huts.	
	30.1.18		Company continued the work of erecting walls round huts.	
	31.1.18		Company continued the work of erecting walls round huts.	

R A Druitt Capt
OC 140 Coy M.G.C.

WAR DIARY
INTELLIGENCE SUMMARY

Army Form C. 2118.

140th Machine Gun Coy.

February 1918

Place	Date	Hour	Summary of Events and Information	Remarks and references to Appendices
BERTINCOURT	1st		The erection of splinter-proof walls round the huts occupied by the Company was continued. The section on anti-aircraft duty had an uneventful day	
	2nd		The sections were engaged on barrage drill and physical training. There was no enemy aircraft activity	Operation Order No 40
	3rd		The sections handed off for the purpose of preparing guns and having limbers for the line. Company moved off to carry out relief of 142 Machine Gun Coy. The was carried out at dusk. The relief was very quick. Casualties NIL	
FLESQUIERES Sector	4th		2 batteries carried out night firing on ORIVAL WOOD K.10.7.5 and K.7.0. 2000 Rounds were fired. Casualties NIL	
	5th		The same batteries again fired 2,000 rounds at night. Targets SE corner of ORIVAL WOOD. Casualties NIL	
Rd. to MOEUVRES	6th		Dispositions unchanged. No night firing. Casualties nil	
	7th		Dispositions unchanged. Casualties nil	
	8th		Dispositions unchanged. Casualties nil	
	9th		Dispositions unchanged. Casualties nil	
	10th		At dawn the forward guns were relieved by the teams which had been on duty overnight. (This work was taken over entirely by the teams forward, and other positions were relieved in the same way)	O.O. No A
	11th		Casualties nil	
	12th		The relief of G. Battery dug outs to note completed. H Battery changed position for a more forward one, for the purpose of firing on FLESQUIERES. The Reserve Section (Anti Aircraft) to making positions. Casualties NIL	
	13th		Dispositions unchanged. Casualties NIL.	
	14th		1 Officer rejoined. 1 OR evacuated sick. Casualties NIL	
	15th		Company was relieved in the line by the 117th M.G. Coy at dusk. The relief was delayed some few hours by roads being shelled with gas & H.E. Casualties 1 OR slightly wounded. The Company assembled at TRESCAULT. Guides then entrained for BERTINCOURT	

Army Form C. 2118.

WAR DIARY
or
INTELLIGENCE SUMMARY.

(Erase heading not required.)

140th Machine Gun Coy
February 1918

Place	Date	Hour	Summary of Events and Information	Remarks and references to Appendices
BERTINCOURT	16th		6 OR rejoined	
	17th		Working party supplied to carry on with new Battalion trench lines.	
	18th		OR/O.R were fitted out with rifles in place of the revolvers which they had previously carried. 1650 rounds were fired at E.A. 6pm 9pm. Signallers, Rangefinders, and No.1-2+3 only, retaining revolvers. Also all P.H. Helmets were handed in.	
	19th		1 officer and 2 OR injured. 20 OR inoculated	
	20th		20 OR were inoculated	
	21st		1 OR accidentally wounded through a live round exploding in fire	
	22nd		1 officer and 3 OR rejoined	
	23rd		Company marched from BERTINCOURT to Hut at KNIGHTBRIDGE BARRACKS, ROCQUIGNY 0.32.d The Machine Gun Companies of the Division assemble here for the purpose of amalgamation into a Divisional Machine Gun Battalion, a travelling cooker was allotted to this unit. 1 officer and 3 other ranks rejoined	
ROCQUIGNY	24th		The four Machine Gun Companys of the Division paraded for Church Service as a Battalion.	
	25th		The Companies are carrying out their training independently. Several Extra huts are being rapidly erected.	
	26th		The Company carried out Machine Gun and Physical Training	
	27th		The Company carried out Machine Gun Tranq Special attention being given to Range Discipline	
	28th		The Company carried out firing Practices on Range in N16 d+d	

G.A. Drake Capt.

Positions of Guns Manned under the Winter Scheme in the Right Brigade Sector handed over by 140th Coy M.G.C. to 142nd Coy M.G.C.

F1 old number MB1d position C.25c 12.32
F2 Temporarily at MB1a position H.6.b 18.45
    to be moved eventually to C.19c 07.10
F3 Temporarily at position B.24d 45.15
    to be moved eventually to C.19c 16.61

S1 old number S2 position B.30c 50.62
THAMES BATTERY at B.30a 2.7. occupied by 140th Coy.
R4   B.29a 05 60
R5   B.29a 08 65

Unoccupied Positions
R1 at H.5a 80.60 } temporarily occupied by
R2   H.5a 55.65 }   Infantry.
R3   B.28d 62.82
R6   B.27a 10.60

Abandoned Positions (Old Serial Numbers)
MB1b at H.6.b 20.55   S5 at B.24d 05.41
S1   B.30c 52.65   S6 at B.24d 17.68
S3   B.30a 58.50
S4   B.30a 60.60

13.11.17.

C.H. Descott Capt
Comdg 140th Coy M.G.C.

SECRET

Operation Order No. 110 by Major R.E.S. Nurse, M.C.
Commanding 140 Machine Gun Company

Ref. Maps. MOEUVRES.   Copy No. 2

1. The 140th Coy. M.G.C. will relieve the 142nd Coy.
M.G.C. in the FLESQUIERES Sector on the night of
the 3/4 inst. in accordance with the table below:—

140	142	Battery	Ref. Map MOEUVRES.
A	D	Reserve	K 28 a 95.80
B	A	G	K 23 d 55.80
D	C	H	K 23 d 62.60
C	B	L	(2 guns) K 23 b 15.80
			(Jump ts at K 18 d 85.80 / 90.85)

Coy. HQ will be at K 29 d 10.60.

2. Guides for the Sections will be met at
K 25 a 80.95 at 5 p.m.
Sections will march at 5 minutes interval in
the order C B D A HQ. Guides for HQ will
be in the Square HAVRINCOURT.

3. Water will be taken up on the night of
relief as follows:—
  A — 9 tins   D — 9
  B — 9 "   HQ — 8
  C — 10 "

On subsequent nights the water cart
will come to the ration Dump, except for the
advanced guns of C Section and Coy HQ, and
water will be fetched from there in tins.
Tins will be taken over from 142nd Coy. for
this purpose, and those taken up from left
will be returned on the night of relief if possible.

4. All Battery Orders and Maps, Belt
Boxes, Gun Boots and other Trench stores
will be taken over and copies of receipts

Operation Orders 1.20 (cont'd)

...forward to Coy HQ by runner...
5. ...Total weight... the other...
by the blue Wood AND YOU

6. Ration Dumps will be as under
   A Lat. K20a 95.35   &C - 1515 a 70.30 (....)
   B,D Lat. K23d 85.90   Coy HQ - K20d 10.05
   &C   K 23c 80.60 (CEMETERY CORNER)

7. ACKNOWLEDGE

Copies to:
 No 1. War Diary
    2. File
    3. A. Coy
    4. B "
    5 & 6. C
    7. D
    8. Transport Officer
    9. 140 Inf. Bde
    10. 142 Coy M.G.C

140 Machine
Gun Company.
Ref. No..............
Date..............

O. ORDER "A"

O.C. Section:-

The following reliefs will take place at dawn on the morning of the 10th inst.

2 guns of A Section under Lieut MANTEGANI will relieve the 2 Forward Guns.

2 guns of A Section under C.S.M. WHITE will relieve L Battery.

B Section under Lieut THOMSON will occupy the new H Battery position in SMILE TRENCH.

C Section will withdraw to the A.A. Battery position as soon as they are relieved by A Section.

C & A Sections will take over all stores & equipment except Guns & Spare Parts.

Stores for H Battery will be carried to the new position as opportunity permits.

O.C's A, B & D Sections will each make arrangements to provide Lieut THOMSON with 4 men at any time after midnight, 8th/9th, for work or carrying as he may require. Arrangements to be made by Lieut. THOMSON direct.

Section Officers

A C
B D

www.ingramcontent.com/pod-product-compliance
Lightning Source LLC
Chambersburg PA
CBHW081548160426
43191CB00011B/1872